Melissa Stewart

W9-CEE-193

BUILDING PEACE

BUILDING PEACE

SUSTAINABLE RECONCILIATION
IN DIVIDED SOCIETIES

JOHN PAUL LEDERACH

UNITED STATES INSTITUTE OF PEACE PRESS
Washington, D.C.

The views expressed in this book are those of the authors alone. They do not necessarily reflect views of the United States Institute of Peace.

UNITED STATES INSTITUTE OF PEACE
1200 17th Street NW, Suite 200
Washington, DC 20036-3011

©1997 by the Endowment of the United States Institute of Peace. All rights reserved.

First published 1997. Fifth printing 2002.

Printed in the United States of America

Library of Congress Cataloging-in-Publication Data
Lederach, John Paul.
        Building peace : sustainable reconciliation in divided societies / John
    Paul Lederach.
            p.   cm.
        Includes bibliographical references.
        ISBN 1-878379-74-7 (hardback). — ISBN 1-878379-73-9 (paperback)
        1. Peace. 2. Pacific settlement of international disputes. 3. International
    relations and culture. I. Title.
    KZ5538.L43 1997
    341.7'3—dc21   97-35584
                                                                                  CIP

For Wendy

*With deep appreciation for your support and encouragement
down the many paths and across the long miles
that the search for peace has taken us*

The delight of building peace?
Like fishing, it is the pursuit of what is elusive,
but attainable,
a perpetual series of occasions for hope.

—Adapted from John Buchan

CONTENTS

● ● ●

FOREWORD

● ● ●

"I have a rather modest thesis," remarks John Paul Lederach in the introduction to this remarkable book. "I believe that the nature and characteristics of contemporary conflict suggest the need for a set of concepts and approaches that go beyond traditional statist diplomacy." Perhaps this thesis is, as the author claims, rather modest, but its implications are certainly not.

The framework that Lederach lays out in this volume with such clarity and sophistication is as ambitious in its breadth and depth as it is in its goal. That goal is the creation in societies currently riven by division and violence of "sustainable peace," by which the author means a good deal more than the already difficult tasks of brokering a cease-fire, negotiating a peace agreement, or implementing a multi-faceted peace accord. Sustainable peace requires that long-time antagonists not merely lay down their arms but that they achieve profound reconciliation that will endure because it is sustained by a society-wide network of relationships and mechanisms that promote justice and address the root causes of enmity before they can regenerate destabilizing tensions. As Lederach notes, this amounts to a "paradigmatic shift" away from the traditional framework and activities that make up statist diplomacy—"away from a concern with the resolution of issues and toward a frame of reference that provides a focus on the restoration and rebuilding of relationships."

The scale and the nature of the changes needed to effect such reconciliation are reflected in the framework with which Lederach conceptualizes contemporary intrastate conflict and the means for its transformation. With a refreshing boldness and breadth of vision, the author argues that all sectors of a society must participate in the building of peace (with "middle-range" rather than "top-level" leaders having a particularly important role to play); that we must address not only the immediate issues in a conflict but also the broader systemic and subsystemic concerns; that conflict is a progression through stages and that peacebuilding is an ongoing process of interdependent roles, functions, and activities; that resources for peace are sociocultural as well as socioeconmic in nature; and that the redefinition and restoration of relationships depends on creating a dynamic, conflict-responsive peacebuilding infrastructure. Lederach also urges that the preparation of people for peacebuilding endeavors be recast, with emphasis given to a process-oriented and context-responsive approach.

This is an ambitious program, to say the least. It goes far beyond the kinds of peacemaking, peacekeeping, and peacebuilding activities we see most frequently: high-profile envoys shuttling between capitals; soldiers in blue berets patrolling streets; nongovernmental organizations (NGOs) delivering food or advice; or even efforts to build civil society or establish rule of law. Each of these activities has a place within Lederach's overall scheme, but each would have to be cast in a new light and be conducted with a different sense of purpose. In Lederach's lexicon, "peacebuilding" does not start and stop with, say, the launch and the termination of a UN operation, or with the establishment of political parties or the holding of elections. Rather, "peacebuilding is understood as a comprehensive concept that encompasses, generates, and sustains the full array of processes, approaches, and stages needed to transform conflict toward more sustainable, peaceful relationships."

This holistic vision is evident throughout *Building Peace,* whether the author is describing the character of contemporary conflict, analyzing the structure of deeply divided societies, or prescribing the means for their peaceful transformation. But how should we, Lederach's readers, respond to so large, so all-encompassing a view?

As Lederach himself anticipates, some critics might be tempted to dismiss his work as well-intentioned but unrealistic. Yet, such a judgment would be superficial. *Building Peace* is a highly sophisticated, intellectually challenging argument from the pen of one of America's leading scholars of conflict resolution. Yet for all his academic credentials, Lederach is most at home putting his ideas into practice. He has spent much of the past fifteen years working with peacebuilding initiatives in such places as Somalia, Colombia, Nicaragua, Northern Ireland, the Philippines, and the Basque region of Spain. Indeed, at the outset of this book he declares that his "thinking and approach emerge from the standpoint of a practitioner rather than a theorist." At the least, given the recent difficulties that the international community has encountered in imposing settlements from the outside, Lederach's argument surely deserves careful consideration: It may well be that external intervention is most effective when it empowers indigenous actors to create a self-sustaining infrastructure of processes that promote reconciliation.

Lederach himself sees this work as an attempt to respond to the nature of contemporary conflict with both innovation and realism. While he urges "the development of ideas and practices that go beyond the negotiation of substantive interests and issues," he asserts the indispensability of "grounded political savvy" and calls for a frank recognition of the "hard-core" quality of intrastate conflicts. The framework presented in *Building Peace* is conceptual in nature, but it has a distinctly practical orientation. In the final chapter of this book, John Prendergast, an executive fellow at the United States Institute of Peace who has worked with governments, intergovernmental organizations, and NGOs, demonstrates how Lederach's theoretical apparatus may be used in real-life situations with a look at four cases of intrastate conflict in Africa.

This book is a substantively reworked and significantly expanded version of a manuscript published by the United Nations University in 1994—a manuscript which was used by the Institute's own Education and Training Program in its work of training professional peacebuilders. The strong response from participants in those programs prompted the Institute to support an expanded and updated version of the original manuscript.

Building Peace complements other published work from the Institute by offering a conceptual counterpart to in-depth studies of specific intrastate conflicts and peace processes (for instance, Richard

Synge's examination of *Mozambique,* John Hirsch and Robert Oakley's assessment of *Somalia and Operation Restore Hope,* and Mohamed Sahnoun's reflections, *Somalia: The Missed Opportunities*) and to more geographically wide-ranging studies (for instance, *Nurturing Peace* by Fen Hampson, *Minorities at Risk* by Ted Gurr, and *African Conflict Resolution,* edited by David Smock and Chester Crocker). This book also adds another perspective to the range of conceptual approaches advanced in Institute publications such as *Peacemaking in International Conflict,* edited by William Zartman and Lewis Rasmussen, *Preventing Violent Conflicts* by Michael Lund, *Autonomy* by Ruth Lapidoth, and *Arts of Power* by Chas Freeman.

These and other publications testify to our wish to bring to the academic and policymaking communities a diversity of potentially useful approaches. This full range of work demonstrates the Institute's commitment to developing theory but even more so to promoting practice. Lederach succeeds in advancing both goals, expanding our understanding of the depth and breadth of effort and involvement needed to bring lasting peace.

Richard H. Solomon, President
United States Institute of Peace

ACKNOWLEDGMENTS

• • •

This book is the result of many experiences, conversations, and collaborative work over the years. It is not possible in a few lines to adequately acknowledge and thank all those who have influenced and contributed to this project. There are, of course, a number of colleagues who deserve special mention.

I appreciate the early encouragement to write this book from Kumar Ruppesinghe, who coordinated the United Nations University's monograph series on Conflict and Governance in which some elements of this book were originally published. My thinking and the content of this book have benefited from my cooperation and work with a number of colleagues over the years, including Cynthia Sampson, Dr. Hizkias Assefa, Dr. Ron Kraybill, Dr. Christopher Mitchell, Juan Gutierrez, and Bill Potapchuk. On the practice side, I have gained enormously from the collaborative work with the Life and Peace Institute and colleagues Sture Normark and Suzanne Lunden and from the Somali members of the Ergada. In recent years the intensive efforts at training with colleagues from the Nairobi Peace Initiative and Justapaz in Bogota, Colombia, have helped formulate the ideas and concepts presented in this book. For their patient prodding and for expanding my horizons, I will always be grateful to my Latin American friends, particularly Dr. Gustavo Parajon, the Rev. Andy Shogreen, Ricardo Esquivia, Zoilamerica Ortega, and Alejandro Benda—a, and to my Irish colleagues, Brendan McAllister, Joe Campbell, and Mari Fitzduff. I have greatly appreciated being able to work with the Education and Training Department of the United States Institute of Peace and for the support for the rewriting of this text from Dan Snodderly, Nigel Quinney, and Lewis Rasmussen. Finally, this text owes a great debt and a second note of thanks to the early, consistent, and brilliant editing by Cynthia Sampson, and to the wonderfully patient staff at the Eastern Mennonite University's Institute for Peacebuilding, including Ruth Zimmerman, Vernon Jantzi, Lynn Quay, Terry Phibbs Witmer, and Cheryl Helmuth.

I am deeply grateful to the United Nations University, particularly the Academic Division and Professor Takashi Inoguchi, Senior Vice Rector, for giving permission to use and reprint here portions of the original monograph *Building Peace*, which was published in 1994 in the United Nations University's series on Conflict and Governance.

INTRODUCTION

● ● ●

Several years ago I attended a series of UN-sponsored national reconciliation conferences addressing the Somali conflict. In one of
those conferences, a close Somali friend, who was participating as a
delegate representing Somali nongovernmental organizations, met
his cousin in the corridor. The cousin was chairman of one of the
key political parties in Mogadishu.

"Mr. Chairman," my friend cajoled his cousin with typical Somali
humor, "how is it that you warlords think that one of you has the
right to be president?" He was referring to the political haggling and
resulting impasse that seemed to set in at every Somali peace conference over what clan, and ultimately what person, would rise to
the presidency. "Don't you know," my friend continued, "that without a frame the roof of a house collapses?"

"You know as well as I," replied the chairman, deftly shifting
metaphors as the Somalis in their oral tradition do so well, both in
poetry and proverb, "the key to a healthy body is a good head. I have
never seen legs walk or arms move without a head."

"Dear cousin," my friend replied with a deep note of sadness, "the
house has collapsed. The legs have been crushed, the arms are bled
clean. There is no body to be head of."

This exchange captures both the dilemma of pursuing peace in
war-torn Somalia and the challenge that faces so many war-ravaged
and violently divided societies around the world. In essence, the
challenge is one of how to build and maintain the house of peace. It
is this challenge I wish to address in the following pages.

My inquiry is based on three primary questions: What is the nature—what are the key characteristics—of contemporary armed conflicts that divide societies across our globe? What are useful concepts and perspectives for building peace in the midst of these conflicts? What are practical approaches and activities that move us toward peaceful and constructive transformation of conflict and have the potential for sustaining that movement?

I have a rather modest thesis. I believe that the nature and characteristics of contemporary conflict suggest the need for a set of concepts and approaches that go beyond traditional statist diplomacy. Building peace in today's conflicts calls for long-term commitment to establishing an infrastructure across the levels of a society, an infrastructure that empowers the resources for reconciliation from within that society and maximizes the contribution from outside. In short, constructing the house of peace relies on a foundation of multiple actors and activities aimed at achieving and sustaining reconciliation. The purpose of this book is to outline a set of ideas and strategies that undergird sustainable peace.

I wish to clarify from the outset that my thinking and approach emerge from the standpoint of a practitioner rather than a theorist. Although there are numerous places throughout this book where theory is employed—where I present ideas about how things work, are related, and can be more clearly perceived by using a variety of lenses—my theoretical endeavors are not aimed at suggesting hypotheses to be tested. My approach is more inductive in nature, representing attempts to bring together lessons learned while facing real-life dilemmas of peacebuilding and mediation. What I wish to bring to the broader discussion of peacebuilding in the international arena are ideas emerging from a practice-oriented learning process.

Accordingly, I draw examples from the regions around the globe where I have had direct experience. In the past fifteen years I have worked in more than twenty countries across five continents, providing training in conflict transformation and a variety of services related to the design and support of peacebuilding initiatives. The framework of this book is strongly influenced by my experiences in Nicaragua as a member of the team that mediated between the Sandinista government and the East Coast indigenous uprising during the late 1980s, by my intensive involvement with the Somali crisis in the early 1990s, and by my longer-term work supporting peace-building efforts in Colombia, Northern Ireland, the Philippines, and the Basque country. In all of these areas, I have functioned chiefly as a nongovernmental actor working in various forms of what is broadly referred to as "second-track diplomacy." My hope is that the basic framework for peacebuilding that this book presents will encourage both practitioners and scholars to reflect on their own experiences and areas of expertise.

The three primary questions on which this book is based also shape its overall structure. The first part of the book is an overview of the characteristics of contemporary conflict, both across our globe and within divided societies. The second part lays out the fundamental perspectives and concepts of peacebuilding that have emerged from direct experience. Part II includes a description of key operational concepts and more specific suggestions about how an approach to sustainable peace can be constructed. The book concludes with a chapter written by John Prendergast, who applies some of the concepts discussed in part II to four instances of contemporary conflict.

PART I

CONTEMPORARY ARMED CONFLICT

Each day, it seems, our morning papers are splashed with headlines announcing another perplexing addition to the dreadful list of unresolved and violent conflicts. Gruesome, explicit photographs accompany the horrid detail of stories of suffering from Bosnia to Rwanda to Burma. We are easily left wondering about the future of our globe. At the same time, though, negotiations are proceeding and peace accords are being signed, from the Middle East to Guatemala. The combination of extensive fighting and a continual search for peace raises interesting questions about where things stand across our globe nearly a decade since the end of the Cold War. Are things better or worse? Have the numbers of wars increased? What is the nature of contemporary armed conflict?

A starting point for addressing these kind of questions—and for discussing peacebuilding—is to understand contemporary armed conflict, its characteristics, and impact. This first part of the book thus provides an overview of armed conflict, focusing on the characteristic features of today's most common form of warfare, intrastate conflict. The purpose of the overview is not to present an exhaustive analysis of the available data on armed conflicts since World War II. Rather, it is to establish a working foundation for a discussion about assumptions, approaches, and mechanisms for dealing with these conflicts from a peacebuilding perspective.

We can capture this big picture by approaching our subject from three angles. First, chapter 1 explores some of the global features of contemporary armed conflict. This includes a look at the geography of where conflicts have taken place, reflections on how they are classified and compared in the academic literature, and finally a discussion of the reasons for their emergence. Second, chapter 2 outlines the more specific nature of these conflicts by examining the key attributes and dynamics that are characteristic of deeply divided societies. Finally, the descriptive overviews provide an opportunity to more clearly articulate the kinds of situations and challenges facing us when we undertake peacebuilding initiatives in contemporary settings of conflict.

1

GLOBAL OVERVIEW

● ● ●

Organized and sustained conflict has fascinated writers since time immemorial. From ancient authors such as the taoist Sun Tzu, through Clausewitz, to modern scientific investigators such as Quincy Wright and Richard Barnet, writers have studied and analyzed the many facets and implications of war.[1]

In the early part of this century, peace research and conflict studies began to emerge as disciplines—a process that was significantly accelerated by two world wars. Among the key tasks for students of these disciplines have been defining terms and categories of study, as well as devising methodologies and determining data appropriate for scientific research. Of particular note for our purposes here have been the efforts to identify and more sharply delineate the criteria used to study armed conflict and warfare.

Early studies by Quaker mathematician Lewis Richardson established precedents for tracking and statistically assessing data for descriptive and comparative purposes.[2] In the 1970s and 1980s, with the establishment of organizations such as the Stockholm Institute of Peace Research (SIPRI) and the Peace Research Institute of Oslo (PRIO) and the work of researchers like Johann Galtung and Kenneth Boulding, more consistent data and more reliable mechanisms for assessing those data became available.[3] In the 1980s and into the 1990s, of special note have been Ruth Sivard's publications on military and social expenditures, the *SIPRI Yearbook 1995*, and the annual "Armed Conflict" reports.[4] Peter Wallensteen and Karin Axell have provided a comprehensive comparison of the data from the late–Cold War and the early post–Cold War periods.[5]

The purpose of these first two chapters is to sketch the defining characteristics and patterns of contemporary armed conflicts that must be taken into account in the development of a peacebuilding framework. This does not require us to conduct an exhaustive review of the data or a statistical analysis of war and arms trade across our globe. It is, however, very useful to begin our discussion by looking at the nature of war and armed conflict at a global level.

As is common practice among other researchers, Wallensteen and Axell have suggested a delineation of categories for assessing armed conflict by death tolls, locality, and issues. Specifically, they provide three subset categories of armed conflict. The first is that of *minor armed conflict,* defined as a conflict between armed forces in which fewer than twenty-five people have died in a given year, and in which at least one of the parties was a state. *Intermediate armed conflict* is defined as a situation in which at least one thousand deaths have occurred over the course of the conflict, with at least twenty-five deaths occurring in a particular year. *War* is reserved to describe a conflict in which at least one thousand deaths have occurred in a given year. *Armed conflict* comprises the total of the three categories. This categorization is widely used by other researchers, albeit with some variation. The "Armed Conflict" reports, for example, define an armed conflict as a conflict that claims more than one thousand lives over its course

When we examine recent data in light of Wallensteen and Axell's categories, the results are rather shocking.

- Between 1989 and 1996, more than seventy wars occurred in sixty locations and involved more than one-third of all member-states of the United Nations.
- As of the time of this writing (January 1997), forty-four conflicts are under way in thirty-nine countries.
- Half of the current wars have been under way for more than a decade, and one-quarter of them for more than two decades.
- Almost two-thirds of the current armed conflicts involve the use of child soldiers under the age of fifteen.

With this categorization and data as a backdrop, let us now examine three aspects of contemporary armed conflict: location, type, and reason.

LOCATION, TYPE, AND REASON

Our purpose here is to understand something more about the global landscape of armed conflicts. One effective mechanism is to visualize the quantified data on a world map. This has been done by a number of authors, including efforts by Johann Galtung and the geographer Tony Ives.[6] More recently, the Carter Presidential Center has published its *State of the World Conflict Report*,[7] and each year the "Armed Conflict" report produces a map of the geography of war.

These maps allow us to stand back and see some of the larger patterns, two of the most notable being patterns of arms exportation and the location of armed conflicts. These visual pictures and the data underlying them lead to a number of important observations. Let us first consider some of the features of the Cold War during the 1980s, and then look at the shifts that are occurring in the post–Cold War period.

The Cold War Era

During much of the Cold War the superpowers were never directly engaged in armed conflict in their own territories. Instead, most wars (well over one hundred in the last fifteen years of the Cold War) were fought through, in, or over client states aligned with the superpowers.

This bipolar context had two effects. In the first place, it suppressed many latent conflicts within the sphere of influence of one or the other of the superpowers; this effect was particularly pronounced in Eastern Europe and Central Asia (for instance, in Armenia, Azerbaijan, and the Balkans). Second, it increased the volatility of, and exacerbated conflicts in, the developing world (as, for instance, in the Horn of Africa and Central America). In the latter case, this created a dominant frame of reference in which the primary explanation for armed conflicts was an ideological struggle between East and West. We thus had a paradox of sorts: the bipolar context served to both *suppress* and *intensify* conflict, depending on the region.

Geographically, the vast majority of wars fought during the Cold War were fought in territories of the periphery, or what is variously termed the "South," the "developing world," and the "two-thirds world." Africa, Southeast Asia, the Middle East, and Latin America: in all of these areas war was by no means uncommon. The Cold War was, for the most part, cold only in Europe and North America. In many parts of the developing world it was in fact very hot.

It is important to note that wars were located in territories housing the most fragile populations—in areas where basic human needs such as housing, health, and education were rarely or barely satisfied.[8] To take one concrete indicator: in ten African countries in 1980–83, more money was spent on military expenditures than on health and education combined.[9] Such indicators help us understand why regions such as the Horn of Africa are today awash with weapons yet have a very fragile social infrastructure. This situation has the potential to create monumental humanitarian disasters, as seen in Somalia in the early and mid-1990s.

During the Cold War the arms trade grew to become a multi-national web of influence—a development with profound geographic ramifications. During the Cold War more than 95 percent of arms exports came from five countries, all located in the North.[10] Imports of weapons, by contrast, moved chiefly into the hot spots in the South. Three straightforward observations can be made about this state of affairs.

First, war has been and continues to be functional for the arms industry. This industry is of economic benefit to the arms-producing countries and individual arms dealers. Second, a very lucrative, multinational, nearly autonomous arms trade industry and market exist that move small arms as well as much larger weapons, from primary to secondary and tertiary markets. Weapons have been and are readily available for any group with sufficient funds. This leads to the third observation—namely, that countries and regions (such as the Horn of Africa) that experienced wars during the Cold War were flooded with weapons from both superpowers. To put all of this in rather crass terms, the Cold War meant that weapons, the loans needed to finance the purchase of weapons, and ideologies came from the North; the South contributed its environments, peoples, and national economies.

The Post–Cold War Era

Wallensteen and Axell's 1993 overview and the 1996 "Armed Conflict" report suggest several important trends in numbers and locations of armed conflict in the early post–Cold War era.

The number of wars counted at the end of each year has remained nearly constant, ranging between thirty-six and forty-four. Each year a number of wars have ended and each year new ones have broken out. As we look more closely at the intermediate and minor conflicts, however, we find two trends.

First, the number of intermediate armed conflicts has remained fairly constant. This suggests that historic conflicts—or what many researchers are now calling "protracted" conflicts—continue to be one of the most challenging obstacles to achieving a truly new and more stable world order. The 1996 "Armed Conflict" report notes that one in four of the forty-four wars in progress has been going on for more than two decades. As Peter Wallensteen noted in a 1993 article,[11] these situations have not been easily resolved in the post–Cold War era, as some theorists predicted they would,[12] nor have a plethora of new wars emerged with the thawing of superpower relations, as others predicted.[13]

This invites examination of why armed conflicts occur. While it is not the purpose of this book to undertake a comprehensive response to this question, it is worth noting for our purposes that during the Cold War the dominant explanation for armed conflict was related to ideological considerations. Certainly, the leaders involved in conflicts knew full well how to play the rhetoric of a particular superpower to their maximum benefit. It is also quite true that ideology, particularly between the superpowers, was very real in its application and consequences given that millions of people actually died. The fact that the post–Cold War era, which has seen the crumbling of animosities between former enemies, has witnessed neither a drastic reduction nor a dramatic increase in the numbers of wars suggests, however, that ideology was not an adequate explanation for the conflicts of the Cold War.

In more recent years, the explanatory buzzword has become "ethnicity" or, in some cases, "religion." Ernie Regehr has rightly pointed out, however, that describing a conflict as ethnic in nature should not be confused with seeking its fundamental sources.[14]

Most current wars are intrastate affairs. The primary issues of contention concern governance and often involve the pursuit of autonomy or self-government for certain regions or groups. At least half of the current wars have to do with the redefinition of territory, state formation, or control of the state.[15] In the popular press these wars are often called "ethnic conflicts," given that what is at issue are group and community rights and not just individual human rights. It is more accurate, therefore, as Mats Friberg has underscored, to name these "identity conflicts" rather than ethnic conflicts, given that there is nothing innately ethnic about them.[16] Rather, it is often the failure of governing structures to address fundamental needs, provide space for participation in decisions, and ensure an equitable distribution of resources and benefits that makes identification with a group so attractive and salient in a given setting. As Regehr has observed:

> Identity conflicts emerge with intensity when a community, in response to unmet basic needs for social and economic security, resolves to strengthen its collective influence and to struggle for political recognition. Almost two-thirds of the current armed conflicts can be defined as identity conflicts, and some estimates count as many as 70 current political conflicts worldwide that involve groups formally organized to promote collective identity issues.[17]

The second numerical trend suggested by the data is the increase of minor armed conflicts in the 1990s.[18] At least two plausible explanations can be advanced to account for this increase, which cannot yet be projected as a pattern. To begin with, the breakup of superpower dominance, in particular the disintegration of the Soviet Union, has apparently eased the Cold War "suppression" effect. In place of one country, the Soviet Union, some fifteen new (or, as others might argue, historic) state boundaries are being drawn, many of which are fostering internal and cross-national conflicts that are defined at this point as minor armed disputes. Some of these have become—and more are likely to shift toward—larger-scale conflicts, even wars, such as occurred in Chechnya. The demise of the Soviet Union has also allowed long-standing animosities in Eastern Europe to come to the fore and provoke bitter conflict, as in the case of the former Yugoslavia.

Another explanation for the increase in the number of minor armed disputes is the growing readiness of various nonstate actors (for instance, guerrilla movements) to regard their use of arms in the pursuit of social and political goals as legitimate. This is certainly the case when social movements and identity groups seek change, yet the political structures within which they operate provide little opportunity for participation and little space for the nonviolent pursuit of their goals.

The years since the end of the Cold War have witnessed shifts not only in the numbers but also in the locations of armed conflicts. The data available from 1989 to 1996 suggest three significant observations about this trend.

First, the majority of wars and protracted intermediate conflicts are still located in the developing countries of the South. An old African proverb has been used to describe the Cold War: "When two elephants fight, it is the grass that suffers." Recently, Professor Ali Mazrui proposed a variant better suited to the post–Cold War era: "When two elephants make love, it is still the grass that suffers." In other words, the thawing of East-West relations has not necessarily ameliorated the plight of the developing world. In fact, the inverse may be true. International aid and attention has shifted toward Eastern Europe and the former Soviet Union, affecting most directly the continents of Africa and Latin America.

Second, there has been a marked increase in armed conflict in Eastern Europe and the former Soviet Union, particularly those parts that touch Central Asia.

Third, there has been a remarkable decline in major armed conflict in Latin America. In part, this decline reflects the progress achieved by regional peace processes (such as that pursued in Central America), which have helped relocate conflicts from battlefields to political arenas (a notable recent example being that of Guatemala). It would seem, however, that these are shifts in degree rather than completed processes of conflict resolution. Nicaragua, for example, does not now appear in the data as a minor conflict, much less as war. Nonetheless, it remains a country with diffuse armed groups creating a volatile, multiparty structure that could easily move toward the minor or even intermediate level of conflict.

CONCLUSION

This brief survey suggests that armed conflicts have taken place mostly on the territories of poorer developing countries. There is an all-too-high but relatively consistent number of major wars and intermediate conflicts across the globe and a rising number of minor armed disputes. Although a significant number of wars have reached a peaceful conclusion, new ones have emerged. For the most part, these conflicts are internal rather than international and feature competition between sharply defined identity groups.

Overall, the challenge for peacebuilding remains monumental. As a global community, we face forty-four wars in nearly as many countries. If we are to address such situations constructively, we must understand with more clarity the nature and characteristics of these conflicts and their settings.

2

CHARACTERISTICS OF DEEPLY DIVIDED SOCIETIES

● ● ●

The previous chapter provided a broad overview of conflict across the globe. We now turn to an examination of common characteristics of deeply divided societies, which are defined here as societies experiencing armed conflict at one of the three levels delineated by Wallensteen and Axell.

The discussion in chapter 1 allows us to identify several starting points for consideration of the characteristics of deeply divided societies.

- The ideological paradigm that was used to consider international conflict in the Cold War is increasingly less salient in explaining the nature of contemporary conflict.

- The vast majority of armed conflicts still take place in the developing world, although an alarming increase in violence has occurred in Eastern Europe and portions of the former Soviet Union.

- In almost all cases, these conflicts are *intranational* in scope, that is, they are fought between groups who come from within the boundaries of a defined state.

- Although most conflicts are intranational in primary composition, they *internationalize* to the degree that some conflictants, particularly opposition movements, inhabit neighboring countries; weapons and money for the conflict flow in from the surrounding region and from more distant locations; and displaced refugee populations cross immediate and distant borders. As such, many contemporary armed conflicts are most accurately defined as *internal and internationalized*.

• Internal and internationalized conflicts contribute to regional, not just national, instability and fighting. In fact, in many instances it is only possible to understand the dynamics and roots of a conflict through a *regional* perspective. This may be especially true in regions such as the Balkans, the Horn of Africa, the Great Lakes region in Central Africa, and the Andean region, where there exists an overlay of armed conflicts that are both subnational and regional.

• Our global community has a long history of legitimating the use of armed force—especially by nation-states—for reasons of security and defense. Weapons production has been and continues to be seen within the overall global system as both legitimate and lucrative. The easy availability of weapons increases the level of violence within a conflict, thus exacerbating the damage sustained by the local civilian population and the environment.

The overall dollar value of weapons traded and purchased has declined since the end of the Cold War, not least because there are today fewer sales of large weapon systems and equipment. However, many contemporary armed conflicts are fought with small arms, not large weapon systems, and the production, trading, and purchasing of small weapons constitute a growing market. Although it is not clear that the availability of arms per se causes conflict, it is clear that access to weapons, particularly light weapons, contributes to the volatility of situations and the capacity of divided groups to sustain armed conflict over long periods.

As we now deepen our examination of these general observations and characteristics, more concrete detail emerges that suggests some patterns across the majority of current conflicts. We can start with the fundamental assertion that intranational conflict, at all three levels, is more akin to communal and intercommunal conflict than to international—that is, interstate—conflict.[1] This assertion emerges from four interactive factors.

1. Cohesion and identity in contemporary conflict tend to form within increasingly narrower lines than those that encompass

national citizenship. In situations of armed conflict, people seek *security* by identifying with something close to their experience and over which they have some control. In today's settings that unit of identity may be clan, ethnicity, religion, or geographic/ regional affiliation, or a mix of these. In worst-case scenarios, this narrowing of identity becomes what was once called the "Leban-onization" and may now be called the "Somalization" of conflict. The consequence is the breakdown of centralized authority and, in some instances, state infrastructure. More importantly, how-ever, the process by which this happens has its roots in long-standing distrust, fear, and paranoia, which are reinforced by the immediate experience of violence, division, and atrocities. This experience, in turn, further exacerbates the hatred and fear that are fueling the conflict.

[margin note: T.V. showing it - visual]

Such a process is common to the sociological dynamics inherent in the progression of conflict at any level. Sociologists have, for example, identified patterns such as the movement from disagree-ment to antagonism to hostility, and the strengthening of a group's internal cohesion in response to the sharpening definition of external threats and enemies.[2] The difference between contem-porary internal conflicts and traditional conceptualization of international conflict is the immediacy of the experience.

This immediacy arises from the close proximity of conflicting groups, the shared common histories of the conflictants, and the dynamic of severe stereotyping coupled with radically differing perceptions of each other. The geographic setting of these conflicts is often the immediate community, neighboring villages, or the domains of close subclans. In the immediacy of such localized settings, which are highly descriptive of the majority of the armed conflicts in the mid-1990s, people seek security in increasingly smaller and narrower identity groups. This, it seems, is why the lines of contemporary armed conflict are increasingly drawn along ethnic, religious, or regional affiliations rather than along ideological or class lines. It is useful to note, however, that both class and ideology often act as underlying forces in the dynamics of control and domination—forces that the leaders of various conflicting groups manipulate to further their positions. In sum, contemporary armed conflicts often occur in situations where identities cut vertically and horizontally through society.

2. These same dynamics help create two other important features: factionalization and diffusion of power. One of the complexities found in many conflict settings is the multiplicity of groups and collectivities vying for recognition and power, often in the form of armed movements. Wallensteen and Axell have identified more than 150 opposition groups around the globe.[3] In the *Horn of Africa Bulletin,* a bimonthly summary of news from the Horn, the acronyms of political parties and movements in Djibouti, Somaliland, Somalia, Eritrea, Ethiopia, and Sudan number as many as one hundred, with shifting names and alliances in evidence nearly each issue.[4]

   Power is diffuse in such settings, and does not operate out of a statist hierarchy. It is diffuse because of the multiplicity of groups, weakened central authority, the shifting of alliances, the autonomous nature of action within alliances and groups by subgroups, and the general dynamic of groups and individuals seeking local influence and control. The consequence of this diffusion is twofold. In the first place, it is never easy to assess the ability of individual leaders either to control the actions of the groups they claim to represent or to deliver their constituencies. Second, it is difficult to identify appropriate mechanisms for establishing representation within a population, and harder still to locate decision-making structures that are not fluid and ephemeral.

3. These conflicts are by nature lodged in long-standing relationships. In other words, they are "protracted"[5] or "intractable."[6] Part of the challenge posed by many armed conflicts is the long-term nature of the conflicting groups' animosity, perception of enmity, and deep-rooted fear. This is coupled with the immediacy of having the enemy living virtually next door, as in many areas of Bosnia, Somalia, Azerbaijan, Rwanda, and Colombia. For the purveyor of inflammatory propaganda, these settings are not a hard sell. The enemy is not halfway around the globe; the enemy lives only a village away, or in some instances next door.

   Thus, critical to the dynamic that drives contemporary conflicts are social-psychological perceptions, emotions, and subjective experiences, which can be wholly independent of the substantive or originating issues.[7] This is part and parcel of the sociological dynamic of "reciprocal causation," where the response mechanism within the cycle of violence and counterviolence becomes the cause for perpetuating the conflict, especially where groups have experienced mutual animosity for decades, if not generations.[8]

Where there is deep, long-term fear and direct experiences of violence that sustain an image of the enemy, people are extremely vulnerable and easily manipulated. The fears in subgroup identities are often created, reinforced, and used by leaders to solidify their position and the internal cohesion of the group behind them. Deep polarization and sharp divisions are, in fact, functional for increasing cohesion, reducing ambiguity, and decreasing internal criticisms of leaders. A clearly defined and immediately present enemy and the perception that the group's survival is at stake inspire uncritical support of the group's leadership. "If we do not dominate, we will be dominated" becomes a leitmotif. Over the years, war is seen by the subgroups and by people on all sides as a fight for survival, in terms both of individual life and of group identity. At the same time, from within the setting, it is difficult for people to see *war as a system* that is oppressive to all involved.

4. So far, we have described the characteristics that are present in conflict situations, externally and internally. We must also identify characteristics that are *not* available or present. In so doing, we must recognize that due to the internal nature of most contemporary armed conflicts, formal and governmental international mechanisms for dealing with conflict are limited. In most countries, and certainly in the founding charters of international organizations such as the United Nations, the Organization of African Unity, and the Organization of American States, there exist specific political and legal restrictions militating against "intervention" in the internal affairs of a member-state. This was, in fact, identified by participants in a conference held by the Carter Center in 1992 as a gap in the response and resources available for dealing with contemporary conflicts.[9]

Contemporary conflict has underscored the reality that in many parts of the world, the identity of people is not organically tied to citizenship in the state, yet the defining paradigm that informs the approaches for understanding and dealing with these conflicts remains that of international—in other words, interstate —diplomacy. Thus, intervention in internal conflicts is restricted not only by the charters of the major regional and international institutions but also by the lack of appropriate and adequate concepts, approaches, and modalities for intervention. We persist in relying on traditional statist diplomacy, despite its inadequacies in responding to the nature of conflicts today.

The history and culture of international diplomacy are rooted in, and emerged out of, the formation of the state system. Yet, at issue in many of today's conflicts is the very nature of existing states, as contested by disputing internal groups. Returning to the key characteristics of armed conflict in divided societies, we can identify a few of the important assumptions on which international diplomacy has traditionally operated and which highlight its inadequacy in the face of intrastate conflict.

A statist approach, for example, assumes that groups in conflict operate according to defined hierarchies of power. The key to dealing with the conflict is seen as a process of identifying and then working with the respective authoritative representatives. Further, at times of war, it may be assumed that political, cultural, and social power are subservient and secondary to, or an outgrowth of, military power. These two assumptions lead to some important strategies of action that can work well where there are clear structures of authority or legitimate processes of establishing representation, but are conceptually inadequate and can in fact exacerbate the situation when those systems are lacking.

In contemporary conflicts, where a multiplicity of fluid groups and alliances exist, and where decision-making power is diffuse, a rigid statist approach is likely to empower a few people who claim representation and have the paradoxical consequence that, to be taken seriously by the international community, a leader must demonstrate a military capacity. This, in large part, may explain the proliferation, in some cases almost overnight, of armed movements vying for recognition.

To take a second example: Traditional diplomacy views armed conflict as primarily motivated and sustained by substantive interests, historically understood as "national interests." Therefore, diplomatic solutions are sought within a framework of compromise on these interests, often within a rather short-term frame of reference. As outlined above, however, the dynamics of intermediate- and war-level conflicts suggest they are equally driven by psychosocial elements—long-standing animosities rooted in a perceived threat to identity and survival. Thus, contested issues of substance (such as territory or governance) are intimately rooted in the cultural and psychological elements driving and sustaining the conflict.

CONCLUSION

The preceding global overview of armed conflict and the key characteristics of deeply divided societies identified in this chapter lead to a number of important conclusions. First is the enormity of the peacebuilding task. Most wars are located in settings on the margins of the world community that are struggling with poverty, inequities, and underdevelopment. The lines of conflict in these settings are typically drawn along group identity lines, with the fighting aimed at achieving collective rights, in opposition to other groups of differing ethnicity, religion, or race. These are long-standing conflicts. The constancy and continuance of intermediate and war levels of armed conflict defy any quick solutions or facile processes for peace.

Second, the Cold War has left a twofold legacy. It has legitimated and institutionalized armed struggle as *the* mechanism for redressing deeply rooted differences, and it has flooded our global community with a surplus of weapons, particularly light arms.

Third, the sharp rise in minor armed conflicts, especially in newly emerging states whose newly defined boundaries may tilt the balance between minority and majority identity groups, raises serious concerns about how to prevent conflicts from spiraling into violence.

Fourth, conflicts in the post–Cold War world are primarily internal and internationalized disputes in which the direct fighting is often akin to communal or intercommunal strife. These conflicts are characterized by deep-rooted and long-standing animosities that are reinforced by high levels of violence and direct experiences of atrocities. As a result, psychological and even cultural features often drive and sustain the conflict more than substantive issues.

These dynamics have consequences. People, when threatened, seek security in narrower, more localized identity groups (this often leads to their conflicts being labeled "ethnic" or "religious"). Factional groups multiply, with power diffused among their leaders; the sense of complexity, randomness, and even chaos increases, and decision making becomes uneven and unpredictable.

Fifth, the international community's ability to respond to these situations is limited. A major shortcoming is the absence of international mechanisms for dealing with internal conflicts; this problem is compounded by diplomatic approaches to conflict resolution that are ill suited to address the nature of contemporary conflict. Unfortunately, we are much better equipped to respond to the humanitarian crises produced by war than we are to deal with the dynamics and root causes that produce those crises.

These observations serve to underline some of the core challenges confronting the peacebuilding agenda that are addressed in part II of this book. First, we must find innovative ways to transform an international culture that is based on poorly developed mechanisms for nonviolent conflict transformation, that has a deep economic commitment to arms production, and that readily accepts the availability of weapons on the world market as legal and legitimate. Second, the peacebuilding task must take into account the long-term horizon of protracted intermediate conflicts and wars, and develop a comprehensive, multifaceted strategy for ending violence and achieving and sustaining reconciliation. This calls for concepts and approaches that deal with the specific nature of contemporary armed conflict. Third, we must acknowledge that war—protracted armed conflict—is a system, a system that can be transformed only by taking a comprehensive approach to the people who operate it and to the setting in which it is rooted. Finally, we must also take up the challenge of how to prevent newly emerging minor armed conflicts from becoming full-scale wars. It to these challenges that we now turn our attention.

PART II

BUILDING PEACE—
A CONCEPTUAL FRAMEWORK

In 1992, UN Secretary-General Boutros Boutros-Ghali produced an important document titled An Agenda for Peace. In it he proposed responsibilities and responses for the United Nations and the international community in dealing with contemporary conflicts. The proposal included four major areas of activity: preventive diplomacy, peacemaking, peacekeeping, and postconflict peacebuilding. His framework suggests that at different times and in diverse contexts a variety of sequential response mechanisms and functions are needed to promote the resolution of conflict and sustenance of peace.

In general terms I concur with the secretary-general's proposal. There are, however, points of difference. For example, I would urge more circumspection in the deployment of military forces; as was demonstrated in Somalia, militarized peace enforcement used as a peacemaking tool in settings of protracted conflict is risky and likely to be counterproductive. However, the most important departure I will make in this book is in the use of the term "peacebuilding." The secretary-general qualifies the use of the term by connecting it exclusively to the postconflict support of peace accords and the rebuilding of war-torn societies. I agree fully that this is an increasingly critical phase to which much attention must be paid.[1]

As indicated in the title of this book, I suggest that "peacebuilding" is more than postaccord reconstruction. Here, peacebuilding is understood as a comprehensive concept that encompasses, generates, and sustains the full array of processes, approaches, and stages needed to transform conflict toward more sustainable, peaceful relationships. The term thus involves a wide range of activities and functions that both precede and follow formal peace accords. Metaphorically, peace is seen not merely as a stage in time or a condition. It is a dynamic social construct. Such a conceptualization requires a process of building, involving investment and materials, architectural design and coordination of labor, laying of a foundation, and detailed finish work, as well as continuing maintenance.

The purpose of part II is to outline a conceptual, analytical framework for putting in motion and sustaining the construction of peace in the context of armed conflict. By "a conceptual framework" I mean a practical way of looking at the peacebuilding endeavor. I do not attempt in these pages to outline and develop a rigorous, scientific scheme of grand theory related to peacebuilding in contemporary conflict. Instead, I put forward a set of ideas and analytical lenses that suggest how conflict transformation *can be understood in contemporary conflict and how features and components of peacebuilding as a social process are defined, are interrelated, and interact. To that degree, my conceptual framework has elements of theory.*

Part II articulates, from the basis of personal experiences in contemporary conflict situations, the frame of reference that I have found useful for approaching and dealing with conflict in deeply divided societies. In its empirical outlines, the framework was first shaped by my experiences in Africa, especially Somalia, and in Central America, in particular, Nicaragua. Where possible, I have added to this empirical basis with an array of examples from other regions and countries. However, this book is not an effort to provide a rigorous and comprehensive study of any given situation.

Conceptually, I understand a framework as providing the general parameters, the boundary outline that helps create meaning and focus; concepts are the more specific ideas and analytical elements that make up the framework. In other words, a framework helps situate things within a context and provides lenses through which we can look at them. Perhaps most important, a framework provides categories in which we can raise questions and think about specific action.

With regard to the challenge of peacebuilding, I propose a conceptual framework that responds to the set of needs and challenges identified in our overview of armed conflicts. In more specific terms, the framework suggests a comprehensive approach to the transformation of conflict that addresses structural issues, social dynamics of relationship building, and the development of a supportive infrastructure for peace. I envision the framework as containing a set of interrelated yet distinct components. These include structure, process, relationship, resources, and coordination. In the chapters that follow I lay out an overview of the peacebuilding framework by describing each of these components and their corresponding relevant concepts in more detail. Further, suggestions are offered as to how these ideas might be implemented—that is, concrete proposals are made for possible types of action, both in the field of training for peacebuilding and in the practice of peacebuilding. At various points, references are made to real-life efforts and initiatives that illustrate these ideas.

3

RECONCILIATION:
THE BUILDING OF RELATIONSHIP

● ● ●

Subsequent chapters outline the components that make up a peace-building framework. Some of these chapters deal with structural concerns about how the population affected by the conflict can be envisioned and how the emerging "hot" issues are understood. Other chapters present a long-term perspective of conflict as a progression and peacebuilding as a process of integrated roles, functions, and activities. If these were the only elements necessary to build peace, it would seem that this challenge could be tackled by following a mechanical formula: With the right plan in mind and the right materials, skills, and resources in hand, peace would just fall into place! But anyone who has lived in settings of protracted conflict or engaged in peacemaking activities in divided societies knows that standardized formulas do not work. What we must acknowledge and address from the start of our discussion are the uniquely human dimensions of the types of conflict under consideration.

If we recall from our opening survey, many of the key character-istics of contemporary conflict follow from their internal nature. Conflicting groups live in close geographic proximity. They have direct experience of violent trauma that they associate with their perceived enemies and that is sometimes tied to a history of griev-ance and enmity that has accumulated over generations. Paradoxi-cally, they live as neighbors and yet are locked into long-standing cycles of hostile interaction. The conflicts are characterized by deep-rooted, intense animosity; fear; and severe stereotyping.

These dynamics and patterns, driven by real-life experiences, subjective perceptions, and emotions, render rational and mechanical processes and solutions aimed at conflict transformation not only ineffective but also in many settings irrelevant or offensive. To be at all germane to contemporary conflict, peacebuilding must be rooted in and responsive to the experiential and subjective realities shaping people's perspectives and needs. It is at this very point that the conceptual paradigm and praxis of peacebuilding must shift significantly away from the traditional framework and activities that make up statist diplomacy.

I believe this paradigmatic shift is articulated in the movement away from a concern with the resolution of issues and toward a frame of reference that focuses on the restoration and rebuilding of relationships.[1] This calls for an approach that goes beyond a mechanical strategy. The framework must address and engage the relational aspects of reconciliation as the central component of peacebuilding.

A CONCEPTUAL FRAMEWORK FOR RECONCILIATION

Over the years, in what might be called "corridor conversations," I have heard some bickering between two professional communities, the fields of International Relations and of Conflict Resolution. At times it almost sounds like a spat between two siblings, an older brother and a younger sister, who situate themselves along a rather odd continuum that runs from "realism" to "emotionalism."

The big brother, International Relations, trained in political science and with experience in the trenches of international conflict, has tended to see himself as needing to deal with the hard politics of the real world. He sees his younger sister as at best well-intentioned, at worst soft and driven by sentimentalism, and for the most part irrelevant. He finds himself constantly telling her, "Listen, touchy-feely is good for the glee club, but it holds no answers for the big time. We are dealing with hard-core gangsters out there." In contemporary conflict situations, he does not have to go far to find examples of who and what he is talking about.

For her part the younger sister, Conflict Resolution, has tended to see the big brother as locked into power paradigms and unable to reach the root of problems in creative ways. Having been trained in social psychology and influenced by the helping professions, she sees herself as integrating the emotional and substantive concerns in the resolution of conflicts. She finds herself repeating, "Mediators are not marshmallows, you know." She does not have to go far to find child-soldiers abducted into killing to make the case that more than hard politics is needed to support sustainable transformation and change in the society.

This is perhaps a caricature. In fact, for several reasons the dialogue has become less disdainful in recent years. Individuals such as Harold Saunders and Joseph Montville[2] who have worked in the realpolitik of international relations from within formal government structures have sought to engage both communities in constructive dialogue. Meanwhile, the conflict resolution field has grown in size and legitimacy, bolstered by increased research and an expanded range of experience. At the same time, too, the very nature of contemporary conflict has demanded realism and innovation of both communities.

This need for critical innovation tempered by realism demands our attention. Contemporary conflicts necessitate peacebuilding approaches that respond to the real nature of those conflicts. While contemporary conflicts are indeed hard-core situations—the "real politics" of hatred, manipulation, and violence—and require grounded political savvy, traditional mechanisms relying solely on statist diplomacy and realpolitik have not demonstrated a capacity to control these conflicts, much less transform them toward constructive, peaceful outcomes. Contemporary conflict thus demands innovation, the development of ideas and practices that go beyond the negotiation of substantive interests and issues. This innovation, I believe, pushes us to probe into the realm of the subjective—generationally accumulated perceptions and deep-rooted hatred and fear.

In dealing with the challenge posed by contemporary conflict, an important meeting point between realism and innovation is the idea of *reconciliation*. A fundamental question is how to create a catalyst for reconciliation and then sustain it in divided societies. As a starting point it is useful to articulate three working assumptions that I would propose undergird a conceptualization of reconciliation. ① First and foremost is the perhaps self-evident but oft-neglected notion that *relationship* is the basis of both the conflict and its long-term solution. This was well articulated by Harold Saunders and Randa Slim, who put forward relationships as the focal point for sustained dialogue within protracted conflict settings.[3] This approach, though simple in its orientation, has wide-ranging ramifications: Reconciliation is not pursued by seeking innovative ways to disengage or minimize the conflicting groups' affiliations, but instead is built on mechanisms that engage the sides of a conflict with each other as humans-in-relationship.

Lest we regard this as merely the soft thinking of a peace-oriented conciliator, let me add that cutting-edge developments in the new sciences arrive at much the same conclusion about the way the physical world operates. Both quantum and chaos theory strongly indicate that we are ill advised to focus our attention on the parts of a system. Rather, we must look at the system as a whole and to the relationships of its parts if we are to understand its dynamic and structure. Relationships, it is argued, are the centerpiece, the beginning and the ending point for understanding the system.[4] This, I believe, is the essential contribution brought by reconciliation as a paradigm.[5] It envisions protracted conflict as a system and focuses its attention on relationships within that system.

② Second, engagement of the conflicting groups assumes an *encounter*, not only of people but also of several different and highly interdependent streams of activity. Reconciliation must find ways to address the past without getting locked into a vicious cycle of mutual exclusiveness inherent in the past. People need opportunity and space to express to and with one another the trauma of loss and their grief at that loss, and the anger that accompanies the pain and the memory of injustices experienced. Acknowledgment is decisive in the reconciliation dynamic. It is one thing to *know*; it is yet a very different social phenomenon to *acknowledge*. Acknowledgment through hearing one another's stories validates experience and feelings and represents the first step toward restoration of the person and the relationship.

At the same time, reconciliation must envision the future in a way that enhances interdependence. In all contemporary internal conflicts, the futures of those who are fighting are ultimately and intimately linked and interdependent. Opportunity must therefore be given for people to look forward and envision their shared future. The perspective of native peoples, such as the Mohawk nation, is highly instructive in this respect. In the midst of the 1991 Oka crisis, which involved the Mohawk nation and the Quebec and Canadian governments, a Mohawk chief reflected on the decisions before his people. He noted that, as required by Mohawk tradition, the chiefs must think in terms of seven generations. The decisions made seven generations ago affect the Mohawk people today. The decisions made today will affect the next seven generations. Such a long view brings both a sense of responsibility for, and a new clarity about, the shared future.

Reconciliation, in essence, represents a place, the point of encounter where concerns about both the past and the future can meet. Reconciliation-as-encounter suggests that space for the acknowledging of the past and envisioning of the future is the necessary ingredient for reframing the present. For this to happen, people must find ways to encounter themselves and their enemies, their hopes and their fears.[6]

3 The third of our working assumptions is that reconciliation requires that we look outside the mainstream of international political traditions, discourse, and operational modalities if we are to find innovation. To explore this idea in more detail, I would like to recount an experience in Central America that helped me formulate my own views about reconciliation. This emerged from a theological perspective.

For a number of years in the 1980s I worked under the auspices of the Mennonite Central Committee throughout Central America as a resource person conducting workshops on conflict resolution and mediation. As an outgrowth of those efforts, I served as an adviser to a religiously based conciliation team that mediated negotiations between the Sandinista government and the Yatama, the indigenous resistance movement of the Nicaraguan East Coast.

As part of its overall role, the conciliation team accompanied Yatama leaders as they returned from exile to their home area and villages, and explained the agreement that had been reached with the Sandinistas. Given the context of war and the deep-rooted animosities that persisted, these were highly charged meetings. At the opening of each village meeting, the Nicaraguan conciliators would read Psalm 85. The psalmist refers to the return of people to their land and the opportunity for peace. In two short lines at the heart of the text (85:10), the Spanish version reads (in translation), "Truth and mercy have met together; peace and justice have kissed."

Hearing these powerful images time and again in the context of a deeply divided society, I became curious as to how the conciliators understood the text and the concepts that form a pair of intriguing paradoxes. At a training workshop with local and regional peace commissions some time later, I had the opportunity to explore this in more detail. We first identified the four major concepts in the phrase: Truth, Mercy, Justice, and Peace. I then asked the participants to discuss each concept as if it were a person, describing the images it brought to mind, and what each would have to say about conflict.

When discussing the images of Truth, the participants suggested honesty, revelation, clarity, open accountability, and vulnerability. "We see each other as we are," one commented. "Without the person of Truth, conflict will never be resolved. Yet Truth alone leaves us naked, vulnerable, and unworthy."

On Mercy, images emerged of compassion, forgiveness, acceptance, and a new start. This is the idea of grace. Without the person of Mercy, healthy relationships would not be possible. Without compassion and forgiveness, healing and restoration would be out of the question. Yet, Mercy alone is superficial. It covers up. It moves on too quickly.

Justice raised powerful images of making things right, creating equal opportunity, rectifying the wrong, and restitution. "Without justice," one person commented, "the brokenness continues and festers."

With Peace came images of harmony, unity, well-being. It is the feeling and prevalence of respect and security. But, it was observed, peace is not just for a few, and if it is preserved for the benefit of some and not others it represents a farce.

As a conclusion we put the four concepts on paper on the wall, as depicted in figure 1. When I asked the participants what we should call the place where Truth and Mercy, Justice and Peace meet, one of them immediately said, "That *place* is reconciliation."

What was so striking about this conceptualization was the idea that reconciliation represents a social space. Reconciliation is a locus, a place where people and things come together.

Let's think for a moment of how the core concepts in the psalmist's paradoxes might be formulated in terms of contemporary conflict. *Truth* is the longing for acknowledgment of wrong and the validation of painful loss and experiences, but it is coupled with *Mercy*, which articulates the need for acceptance, letting go, and a new beginning. *Justice* represents the search for individual and group rights, for social restructuring, and for restitution, but it is linked with *Peace*, which underscores the need for interdependence, well-being, and security. Curiously, these concepts are played out in the political arena. For example, in El Salvador and Guatemala we can see push and pull of the seemingly contradictory social energies played out in the Truth Commission, on the one side, and the amnesty programs, on the other side. Reconciliation, I am suggesting, involves the creation of the social space where both truth and forgiveness are validated and joined together, rather than being forced into an encounter in which one must win out over the other or envisioned as fragmented and separated parts.

These elements lie at the heart of the challenge facing us in contemporary conflict. Although enormous pain and deep-rooted animosity accompany any war, the nature of contemporary settings of armed conflict—where neighbor fears neighbor and sometimes family member fears family member, and where each sheds blood—makes the emotive, perceptual, social-psychological, and spiritual dimensions core, not peripheral, concerns. The immediacy of hatred and prejudice, of racism and xenophobia, as primary factors and motivators of the conflict means that its transformation must be rooted in social-psychological and spiritual dimensions that traditionally have been seen as either irrelevant or outside the competency of international diplomacy. Reconciliation, seen as a process of encounter and as a social space, points us in that direction.

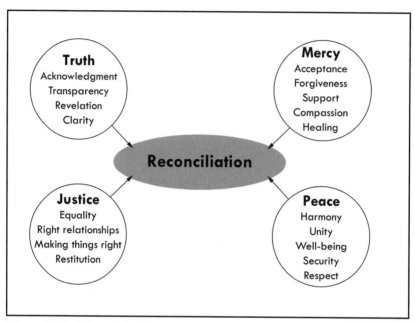

Figure 1. The Place Called Reconciliation.

Reconciliation can be thus understood as both a *focus* and a *locus*. As a perspective, it is built on and oriented toward the relational aspects of a conflict. As a social phenomenon, reconciliation represents a space, a place or location of encounter, where parties to a conflict meet. Reconciliation must be proactive in seeking to create an encounter where people can focus on their relationship and share their perceptions, feelings, and experiences with one another, with the goal of creating new perceptions and a new shared experience.

As such, reconciliation is built on paradox, that which links seemingly contradictory but in fact interdependent ideas and forces. Kenwin Smith and David Berg have suggested that paradoxes are a natural part of group life.[7] To deal with them constructively it is necessary to identify the opposing energies that form the poles of the paradox, provide space for each, and embrace them as interdependent and necessary for the health of the group. In the case of contemporary conflict, the poles of energy, often seen as incompatibilities, are the fundamental human and relational needs inherent in the context of protracted, violent conflict. Reconciliation thus represents the space, or creative tension, that holds these needs and the energy that drives them together.

In more specific terms, reconciliation can be seen as dealing with three specific paradoxes. First, in an overall sense, reconciliation promotes an encounter between the open expression of the painful past, on the one hand, and the search for the articulation of a long-term, interdependent future, on the other hand. Second, reconciliation provides a place for truth and mercy to meet, where concerns for exposing what has happened *and* for letting go in favor of renewed relationship are validated and embraced. Third, reconciliation recognizes the need to give time and place to both justice and peace, where redressing the wrong is held together with the envisioning of a common, connected future.

Reconciliation suggests that the way out these paradoxes is to embrace both sources of energy. A paradox can create a binding and crippling impasse when only one of the sources is embraced at the expense of the other—in other words, groups lock into one element in opposition to the other.[8] The basic paradigm of reconciliation, therefore, embraces paradox. It suggests, for example, that a focus on relationship will provide new ways to address the impasse on issues; or that providing space for grieving the past permits a reorientation toward the future and, inversely, that envisioning a common future creates new lenses for dealing with the past.

THE PRAXIS OF RECONCILIATION

We now return to the question of how to spark and sustain the process of reconciliation in practical terms. It is striking that the field of peacebuilding and conflict transformation is still in its infancy in developing this application, both conceptually and practically. We can, however, point to a number of approaches that have been tried and to some specific experiences that fall within the conceptual paradigm of reconciliation as described above.

There are, for example, grassroots cases from within war-torn Bosnia, where efforts by local Franciscan and Muslim clerics led to communities joining together across the lines of conflict to pursue and sustain local cease-fires.[9] At the level of middle-range leaders in conflicted societies we can instance the growing body of experience of dialogue groups and problem-solving workshops, which have brought adversaries together to explore their experiences and view-points and build relationships, from contexts as varied as Europe, the Middle East, and Africa.[10] To look at the application of some of these ideas about reconciliation, we can explore the microdynamics of the early stages by which the peace accord between Israel and the Palestine Liberation Organization (PLO) emerged, a process that involved elements of the two populations' middle-range leadership, although it also involved top-level leaders.

The signing of the Israeli-PLO peace agreement, televised live from the lawn of the White House, was heralded as one of the most hopeful moments of 1993. Behind the scene of the very public Arafat-Rabin handshake was the story of an agreement delivered by means of what became known as the "Norwegian channel" or the "Oslo channel."[11]

At the time of this writing, we do not yet have a full account of the back-channel process. We do have numerous written accounts in which interviews with the initiators and brokers of the Norwegian channel reveal a fascinating process of risky, individual effort coupled with innovative ways of creating space for intimate encounters.[12]

In brief, two Israeli "peaceniks" initiated what were considered at the time to be illegal contacts with the PLO director of finance, Abu Alaa. These eventually led to secret talks between Palestinians and Israelis in Norway over the course of nearly a year. Terje Rød Larsen, a Norwegian scholar, and his wife Mona Juul, a member of Norway's Foreign Ministry, were key figures in hosting and mediating the talks. For our purposes here, the process that unfolded is of more interest than the substance of the agreement. Several points stand out.

1. The contacts and discussions were held in almost complete secrecy. Only a handful of people within the PLO and the Israeli and Norwegian governments were aware of their existence. Even at the time the agreement was announced, the process and progress of the discussions were virtually unknown and kept carefully out of the public eye.

2. The contacts and early discussions were held between people who had access to top-level officials, but who did not belong to the top level themselves. At later points, when more formal proposals emerged, higher-level representatives became directly involved. In terms of the model used in this book (see chapter 4), while the process was publicly announced at the top level, it was built out of elements of a middle-range initiative.

These first two points underscore a key dilemma in peacebuilding: how to coordinate diverse but related activities at different levels of the affected society. The confidentiality needed to protect the initial stages for those leaders stepping out to explore new possibilities would at a later phase be viewed with great suspicion, and even outright hostility, by those among the Israeli and Palestinian publics who felt left out of the process.

3. Larsen and Juul did everything possible to create an intimate atmosphere. "We wanted them to feel easy in a pleasant house," they reported.[13] The participants stayed in a summer lodge, slept under the same roof, and took all of their meals together. They were, as Jane Corbin wrote, "living, eating, and above all working together."[14] Relationships developed in new, different, and more holistic ways. The participants did not relate to one another exclusively as enemies or political adversaries; rather, they shared time and space and came to see one another as individuals as well as antagonists.

4. Sessions were long and intense, lasting at times up to eight hours and late into the night. Early on, after a round of reciting past histories that invoked mutual recriminations, Abu Alaa set an important tone. "Let us not compete on who was right and who was wrong in the past," he is reported to have said. "And let us not compete about who can be more clever in the present. Let us see what we can do in the future."[15] It would seem that the intimacy of living together provided a transparency of feelings and viewpoints, and the focus on the future permitted the participants to use new lenses for looking at old problems.

5. It took seven meetings over five months before the ground was sufficiently prepared to "upgrade" the level of participation. Israeli

deputy foreign minister Yosi Beilin commented that "we'd never really had any contacts with the PLO . . . we didn't really know what they stood for . . . we knew the propaganda. We did not know the truth."[16] The main contribution made by the middle-range players was that "they prepared the practical and psychological ground that enabled the professionals to join them after the seventh meeting."[17]

This example highlights the importance of developing relationship —of providing a space for the parties to encounter and engage each other as people and a place where they can express feelings openly while also recognizing their shared future. The process, which in this instance enabled a breakthrough to be made in negotiations, was built on a number of the core conceptual elements identified above under the rubric of reconciliation.

The Norwegian channel did not minimize or disregard the need to develop a framework for a negotiated settlement on substantive issues. It did, however, clearly attest to the need for a paradigm of reconciliation as a tool for developing relationship and as part of the microdynamics that became crucial for sustaining the discussions.

At a broader level, efforts to obstruct implementation of the formal Israeli-PLO peace agreement have shown that a comprehensive approach to peacebuilding in the Israeli-Palestinian context is as needed today as it was before. As subsequent chapters explore, we need to examine how to integrate a reconciliation paradigm at the middle-range and grassroots levels on both sides of the conflict. Unless that can be accomplished, the innovation and progress made at the highest level of the peace process will always remain under severe stress and in danger of outright collapse.

CONCLUSION

In this chapter we have explored the promise and the challenge of reconciliation. Reconciliation, we have seen, is focused on building relationship between antagonists. The relational dimension involves the emotional and psychological aspects of the conflict and the need to recognize past grievances and explore future interdependence.

Reconciliation as a locus creates a space for encounter by the parties, a place where the diverse but connected energies and concerns driving the conflict can meet, including the paradoxes of truth and mercy, justice and peace.

Reconciliation as a concept and a praxis endeavors to reframe the conflict so that the parties are no longer preoccupied with focusing on the issues in a direct, cognitive manner. Its primary goal and key contribution is to seek innovative ways to create a time and a place, within various levels of the affected population, to address, integrate, and embrace the painful past and the necessary shared future as a means of dealing with the present.

4

STRUCTURE:
LENSES FOR THE BIG PICTURE

● ● ●

RECONSIDERING THE AFFECTED POPULATION

In the introduction to this book I referred to a conversation between two Somali friends over how the house of peace should be built in their war-torn homeland. One argued that the head needed to be established in order for the body to function. The other suggested that the foundation of the house had to be laid if the roof was to be held up.

Their argument, in essence, involved opposing theories about how to understand and approach the building of peace within a population. Using a mixed metaphor, one argued that peace is built from the top down. The second suggested that it is constructed from the bottom up. Both assumed certain things about the process and affected population in the conflict. Before arriving at any conclusions about which approach is appropriate—or, as the case is made in this book, about how they are integrated and related—we must first develop an analytical framework for describing the levels of an affected population.

I have found it helpful to think of leadership in the population affected by a conflict in terms of a pyramid (see figure 2). An analytical perspective, such as the one proposed here, will always rely to some degree on broad generalizations that provide a set of lenses for focusing in on a particular concern, or for considering and relating a set of concepts. In this instance, we are using lenses to capture the overview of how an entire affected population in a setting of internal armed conflict is represented by leaders and other actors, as well as the roles they play in dealing with the situation. The pyramid permits us to lay out that leadership base in three major categories: top level, middle range, and the grassroots.

We can use the pyramid as a way of describing the numbers within a population in simplified terms. The pinnacle, or top-level leadership, represents the fewest people, in some instances perhaps only a handful of key actors. The grassroots base of the pyramid encompasses the largest number of people, those who represent the population at large. On the left-hand side of the pyramid are the types of leaders and the sectors from which they come at each level. On the right-hand side are the conflict transformation activities that the leaders at each level may undertake. Each of these levels deserves further discussion before we look at the broader implications of the pyramidal model for our conceptual framework.

LEVELS OF LEADERSHIP

Level 1: Top-Level Leadership

Level 1 comprises the key political and military leaders in the conflict. In an intrastate struggle, these people are the highest representative leaders of the government and opposition movements, or present themselves as such. They are at the apex of the pyramid, the spokespersons for their constituencies and for the concerns that, they argue, generate and will resolve the conflict. It is crucial to recognize that in most instances they represent a few key actors within the broader setting. Certain features are common to this level of leadership.

First, these leaders are highly visible. A great deal of attention is paid to their movements, statements, and positions. They receive a lot of press coverage and air time. In some instances, in this era of CNN worldwide news, these leaders find themselves elevated from virtual obscurity to international prominence and even celebrity status. One could argue that this media dynamic possesses a symbiotic and dialectic nature that is related to the legitimacy and pursuit of top-level leaders' personal and political ambitions.[1] A legitimate

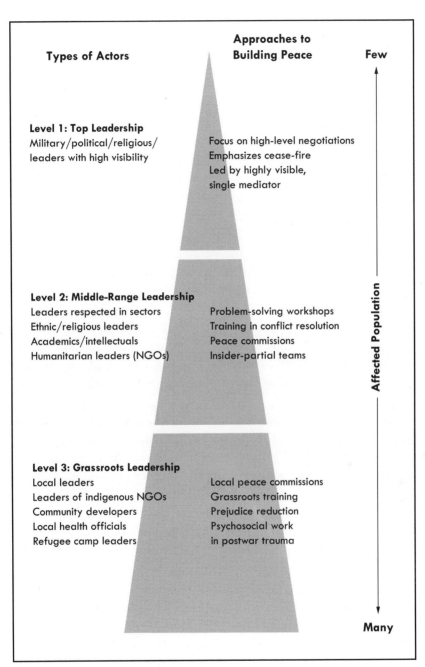

Figure 2. Actors and Approaches to Peacebuilding.

base of representation for a constituency or a set of concerns establishes a leader as such. Publicity and profile are essential for establishing the concerns of that constituency, yet the focus of the publicity is on the leader. Such publicity and profile further consolidate and maintain a leader's base and legitimacy. Visibility and profile thus become essential components descriptive of this level, and they are actively sought by this level, both to represent the concerns of a leader's constituency and to secure his or her own position of influence.

Second, by virtue of their high public profile, these leaders are generally locked into positions taken with regard to the perspectives and issues in conflict. They are under tremendous pressure to maintain a position of strength vis-à-vis their adversaries and their own constituencies. (By "position" we refer here to the almost static viewpoints about solutions that are demanded by each side in order to resolve the conflict.)[2] This, coupled with a high degree of publicity, often constrains the freedom of maneuver of leaders operating at this level. Acceptance of anything less than their publicly stated goals or demands is seen as weakness or loss of face. For the leaders this means that every move represents a high-stakes decision for both their careers and the stated goals of their government or movement.

Finally, these leaders are perceived and characterized as having significant, if not exclusive, power and influence. Certainly, top leaders as individuals do tend to have more influence and power than other individuals. Equally, however, the picture is more complex than initially meets the eye. On the one hand, top leaders benefit from visibility and publicity, and their statements do carry enormous weight, both in the framing of issues and processes and in decision making. On the other hand, in international affairs in general and in protracted settings of conflict in particular, power is primarily perceived in the form of a hierarchy in which top leaders are in a position to make decisions for, and to deliver the support of, their respective constituencies. I say "perceived" because the international community most often seeks out and relates to hierarchical leaders on all sides of an internal conflict as if they had exclusive power, even when, as is often the case, power may be far more diffuse and fractionated. In situations such as Bosnia, Somalia, and Liberia, the degree to which hierarchical power is operational is decidedly unclear. There are many leaders at different levels of the pyramid who may not fall in line behind the more visible leaders. In these situations, action is often pursued and taken in far more diffuse ways within the society, even though any peace accords that may be negotiated assume hierarchical representation and implementation.

Level 2: Middle-Range Leadership

In the middle range are persons who function in leadership positions within a setting of protracted conflict, but whose position is defined in ways not necessarily connected to or controlled by the authority or structures of the formal government or major opposition movements.

Middle-range leadership can be delineated along several different lines. One approach is to focus on persons who are highly respected as individuals and/or occupy formal positions of leadership in sectors such as education, business, agriculture, or health. A second approach is to consider the primary networks of groups and institutions that may exist within a setting, such as those linking (formally or otherwise) religious groups, academic institutions, or humanitarian organizations. These networks contain individuals who lead or are prominent within a particular institution—for instance, the head of an important indigenous nongovernmental organization, the former dean of a national university, or a well-known priest in a given region—who may be well recognized and respected within that network or geographic region. A third approach is to concentrate on the identity groups in conflict, and to locate middle-range leaders among people who are well known as belonging to a minority ethnic group, or who are from a particular geographic region within the conflict and enjoy the respect of the people of that region but are also known outside the region. Yet another approach is to focus on people from within the conflict setting but whose prestige extends much farther—for example, a well-known poet or Nobel laureate.

Important features of this level characterize the key actors within it. First, middle-level leaders are positioned so that they are likely to know and be known by the top-level leadership, yet they have significant connections to the broader context and the constituency that the top leaders claim to represent. In other words, they are connected to both the top and the grassroots levels. They have contact with top-level leaders, but are not bound by the political calculations that govern every move and decision made at that level. Similarly, they vicariously know the context and experience of people living at the grassroots level, yet they are not encumbered by the survival demands facing many at this level.

Second, the position of middle-range leaders is not based on political or military power, nor are such leaders necessarily seeking to capture power of that sort. Their status and influence in the setting derives from ongoing relationships—some professional, some institutional, some formal, others matters of friendship and acquaintance. Consequently, middle-range leaders are rarely in the national or international limelight, and their position and work do not depend on visibility and publicity. By virtue of this, they tend to have greater flexibility of movement and action; certainly, they can travel with an inconspicuousness denied to top-level leaders.

Third, middle-range actors tend to have preexisting relationships with counterparts that cut across the lines of conflict within the setting. They may, for example, belong to a professional association or have built a network of relationships that cut across the identity divisions within the society.

In sum, middle-range actors are far more numerous than are top-level leaders and are connected through networks to many influential people across the human and physical geography of the conflict.

Level 3: Grassroots Leadership

The grassroots represents the masses, the base of the society. Life at this level is characterized, particularly in settings of protracted conflict and war, by a survival mentality. In worst-case scenarios, the population at this level is involved in a day-to-day effort to find food, water, shelter, and safety.

The leadership at the grassroots level also operates on a day-to-day basis. Leaders here include people who are involved in local communities, members of indigenous nongovernmental organizations (NGOs) carrying out relief projects for local populations, health officials, and refugee camp leaders. These people understand intimately the fear and suffering with which much of the population must live; they also have an expert knowledge of local politics and know on a face-to-face basis the local leaders of the government and its adversaries.

In many instances, the local level is a microcosm of the bigger picture. The lines of identity in the conflict often are drawn right through local communities, splitting them into hostile groups. Unlike many actors at the higher levels of the pyramid, however, grassroots leaders witness firsthand the deep-rooted hatred and animosity on a daily basis.

Before we turn our attention to the peacebuilding approaches associated with each level, two broad observations should be made about the pyramid population. First, while many of the fundamental conditions that generate conflict are experienced at the grassroots level—for example, social and economic insecurity, political and cultural discrimination, and human rights violations—the lines of group identity in contemporary conflicts are more often drawn vertically than horizontally within the pyramid. From a descriptive standpoint, in most armed conflicts today, identity forms around ethnicity, religion, or regional geography rather than class, creating group divisions that cut down through the pyramid rather than pitting one level against another. Correspondingly, leaders within each level have connections to their "own people" up and down the pyramid and, at the same time, have counterparts within their own level who are perceived as enemies.

Second, there are two important inverse relationships in the conflict setting. On the one hand, a higher position in the pyramid confers on an individual greater access to information about the bigger picture and greater capacity to make decisions that affect the entire population, but it also means that the individual is less affected by the day-to-day consequences of those decisions. On the other hand, a lower position increases the likelihood that an individual will directly experience the consequences of decision making, but reduces the ability to see the broader picture and limits access to decision-making power. These two inverse relationships pose key dilemmas in the design and implementation of peace processes, to which we now turn our attention.

APPROACHES TO PEACEBUILDING

Level 1: Top-Level Approaches

On the right-hand side of the pyramid are various features of, and approaches to, peacebuilding. At the top level we find what we might call the "top-down" approach to peacebuilding. This approach has the following characteristics.

First, the people who emerge as peacemakers, often seen as intermediaries or mediators, are eminent figures who themselves possess a public profile. They are often backed by a supporting government or international organization such as the United Nations, which lies outside the relationships embroiled in the internal conflict. More often than not, actors at this level operate as single personalities.

Second, the goal is to achieve a negotiated settlement between the principal high-level leaders in the conflict. These peacemakers tend to operate as third parties who shuttle between the protagonists. What transpires is a process of high-level negotiations in which top-level leaders are identified and brought to the bargaining table. Getting to the table and setting the agenda for negotiations become guiding metaphors of the peacemaker's work.

By virtue of the players involved, both the intermediaries and the negotiations are typically subjected to close media scrutiny. Yet, a critical aspect of this work is the need to create sufficient trust and flexibility among the protagonists to permit new options to emerge and compromise to take place. This poses a serious dilemma for a negotiation process conducted in a highly visible environment, in which the lead negotiators must maintain publicly articulated goals and demands in order to not be seen as weak yet move toward each other at the table.

Third, the peacebuilding approach at this level is often focused on achieving a cease-fire or a cessation of hostilities as a first step that will lead to subsequent steps involving broader political and substantive negotiations, which in turn will culminate in an agreement creating the mechanisms for a political transition from war to peace.

A number of operative assumptions undergird peacebuilding activity at the top level. It is assumed, for example, that the key to achieving peace lies with identifying the representative leaders and getting them to agree. This presumes that (1) representative leaders *can* be identified; (2) they *will* articulate and advocate, from the perspective of those they represent, the concerns giving rise to the conflict; and (3) they *possess* the power, or at least the influence, to deliver the support of their respective communities for the implementation of any agreements reached. In other words, the model builds on the assumption of a hierarchical, as well as a monolithic, power structure within the setting.

Moreover, the framework is based on a top-down, or what might more aptly be called a "trickle-down," approach to peace. In essence, it is believed that the accomplishments at the highest level will translate to, and move down through, the rest of the population. According to this model, the greatest potential and the primary responsibility for achieving peace resides with the representative leaders of the parties to the conflict. If these leaders can agree, that sets the stage, the framework, and the environment for delivering the rest of society in the implementation of the agreement that will end the war.

Finally, the top-level approach makes some concrete assumptions about the order and time frame for peace. A certain pattern for a phased approach has emerged that can be detected from the recent peace processes in Ethiopia, El Salvador, and Cambodia. It first involves efforts aimed at achieving a cease-fire agreement with military leaders. Next, a process of "national" transition is initiated involving the political leadership in creating a framework that will lead to democratic elections. "Peace" in the early stages hinges on achieving a cease-fire, and in the later stages on broadening and including more sectors of the society. This assumes a step-by-step, issue-oriented, and short-term achievement process engaged in by top-level leaders. Perhaps the most critical assumption, however, is that by and large the other levels of the population wait for the accord to be reached and only then are engaged in its implementation. In other words, it is assumed that the accord will have to be relevant to and capable of practical implementation at the local level, even though in most instances the accord was reached under enormous political pressure and involved compromises on all sides. As we shall see, this scenario contrasts sharply with the kind of peace process envisaged under a more comprehensive framework, which assumes an interdependence of levels that involve multiple tiers of leadership and participation within the affected population and that integrate simultaneous but pace-differentiated activities.

Level 2: Middle-Range Approaches

The middle range offers what might be called a "middle-out" approach to peacebuilding. It is based on the idea that the middle range contains a set of leaders with a determinant *location* in the conflict who, if integrated properly, might provide the key to creating an *infrastructure* for achieving and sustaining peace. To my knowledge, a theory or literature of middle-range peacebuilding as such has not yet been developed. We do, however, have a number of parallel examples to draw upon of middle-range approaches to peace. These fit into three categories: problem-solving workshops, conflict resolution training, and the development of peace commissions.

Problem-solving workshops. Perhaps the most developed activity theoretically and the most thoroughly evaluated for effectiveness and impact (given that few nontraditional peace processes have received enough attention to be formally evaluated) have been problem-solving workshops.[3] These workshops, at times referred to as "interactive problem-solving"[4] or "third-party consultation,"[5] provide a venue for persons who unofficially represent the parties to a conflict to interact in a process of "collaborative analysis" of the problems that separate them.[6] As Christopher Mitchell has summarized, the approach involves

> informal, week-long meetings of the representatives of parties in protracted, deep-rooted, and frequently violent conflict in an informal, often academic, setting that permits the re-analysis of their conflict as a shared problem and the generation of some alternative courses of action to continued coercion, together with new options for a generally acceptable and self-sustaining resolution.[7]

The problem-solving approach has a number of important features that are characteristic of middle-range peacebuilding. First, participants are typically invited because of their knowledge of the conflict and their proximity to key decision makers, but top-level actors are not invited. Mitchell has referred to such participants as opinion leaders—those who are in a position to influence opinion. The workshop is not an exercise aimed at emulating or replacing formal negotiations. It is an exercise aimed at *broadening* participation in the process, as well as the perceptions of the participants, and *deepening* their analysis of the problem and their innovation in seeking solutions.

Second, the workshop is designed to be informal and off the record, which creates an environment for adversaries to interact in ways that their home settings, and certainly public events, would not permit. An environment is established that enables direct interaction with adversaries and encourages the development of relationships, as well as flexibility in looking at the parties' shared problems and possible solutions. The workshop provides a politically safe space for floating and testing ideas, which may or may not prove useful back in real-life settings.

Finally, the third-party component in the workshop provides multiple services. Among its key functions are the convening of the parties, facilitating the meeting, and providing expertise on the analysis of conflict and processes of conflict resolution. The third-party team seeks to provide participants an opportunity for—and an example of—a more effective mode of interaction, and to permit them to look at the conflict through analytical rather than only coercive lenses. It is worth noting that recent peace processes that have captured public attention have featured, behind the scenes, significant and concerted problem-solving efforts that provided support to the negotiators and fed new ideas into the bargaining process. This was the case, for example, with the PLO-Israeli accord signed in 1993, developments in Northern Ireland in the mid-1990s, and the accord in Guatemala signed in 1996.

Conflict resolution training. Training approaches differ from problem-solving workshops in several respects. Training, in the conflict resolution field, generally has two aims: raising awareness—that is, educating people about conflict—and imparting skills for dealing with conflict.[8] In terms of education, training programs are developed to provide participants with an understanding of how conflict operates, the general patterns and dynamics it follows, and useful concepts for dealing with it in more constructive ways. In terms of developing skills, training has the more concrete goal of teaching people specific techniques and approaches for dealing with conflict, often in the form of analytical, communication, negotiation, or mediation skills.

In contrast to the problem-solving workshop, the focus of training is internally rather than externally oriented. For the most part its purpose is to develop the participants' skills, not to deepen their analysis of a given conflictive situation. Because of the focus on processes and skills, training faces the challenge of how best to orient and adapt its effort in a wide variety of contexts and cultures, while still remaining appropriate and helpful.[9]

A problem-solving workshop constitutes a very carefully constructed process of convening and of selecting participants to provide a balance within the proposed format. Middle-range actors are the most appropriate participants for problem-solving workshops, both because they are knowledgeable about the conflict and because they have access to the top policymakers. Training, while perhaps most strategically useful at the middle level, can in fact be appropriately employed at any level or across levels of leadership within a society. In some instances, a training program may be open to participation by any interested parties; in others, it may target or be requested by a particular group; and in yet other instances, trainers may strategically convene a set of participants from within a setting of conflict.

Some illustrations of practical applications will highlight the role middle-range training has played in peace strategies. In the South African context, for example, the Centre for Conflict Resolution (formerly the Centre for Intergroup Studies) has undertaken an extensive training program directed at providing a conceptual framework and skills for dealing with conflict in the postapartheid "New South Africa." In some instances, the organization has trained leaders of political movements such as the African National Congress; in others, it has targeted sectoral actors such as religious and civic leaders; and in a third approach, it has provided training that brought together former antagonists, such as liberation movement leaders and policemen.[10]

Paula Gutlove and other members of the Harvard-based Balkans Peace Project undertook a program of training middle-level leaders across the former Yugoslavia.[11] Here the threefold goal was to create for participants an opportunity to reflect on the experience of the conflict; to deal with the psychological dimensions inherent in their experience of the conflict; and to develop skills for dealing with conflict in alternative ways.

A third example is the vast array of training approaches and events that have emerged in Northern Ireland.[12] In these instances, the training has not only provided skills but also endeavored to identify Irish approaches and experiments for dealing innovatively with the sharp sectarian divisions.

Yet another example is the efforts by the All Africa Conference of Churches, principally in collaboration with the Nairobi Peace Initiative,[13] to combine the roles of convenor and trainer. Middle-range leaders from church communities who found themselves on different sides of conflicts in countries such as Mozambique and Angola were brought together to share their perceptions and experiences of the conflict, analyze their own roles in it, and develop approaches for encouraging and supporting reconciliation in their context.[14]

What these approaches suggest is that although training is generally thought of as the dissemination of knowledge and imparting of skills, it becomes a strategic tool as it promotes the development of peacebuilding capacities within the middle-range leadership. This potential is further enhanced when training, serving a convening function, brings together people from the same level of society but on different sides of the conflict.

Peace commissions. The third category of middle-range peacebuilding activity involves the formation of peace commissions within conflict settings. These commissions have been as varied in form and application as their settings. Two situations will illustrate the point: Nicaragua in the late 1980s, and South Africa in the early 1990s.

Throughout the 1980s, multiple internal wars raged in Central America. In an innovative approach that built upon the efforts of the earlier Contadora peace process, the Central American peace accord, which was signed in Esquipulas, Guatemala, by the five countries in the region, provided mechanisms that dealt with the internal situations of each country but did so simultaneously, through a coordinated plan.[15] Among the provisions of the plan was a process whereby each country would establish a national peace commission made up of four prominent individuals representing different sides of the conflict. The Nicaraguan government moved quickly, not only to set up its national commission but also to devise a more extensive internal structure that included region-specific commissions and an extensive network of local commissions.[16]

The most extensive of the regional efforts within the country was the establishment of a conciliation commission to deal with the East Coast of Nicaragua. The commission was established to prepare and then facilitate the negotiation and conciliation efforts between Yatama (the umbrella organization of the East Coast indigenous resistance) and the Sandinista government. The conciliation commission was composed of the top leadership of two Nicaraguan religious networks: the Moravian church, which had its roots in the East Coast; and the Evangelical Committee for Aid and Development (CEPAD), an ecumenical arm of the Protestant churches that was based in Managua.[17]

The model for this conciliation effort was that of an insider-partial mediation effort.[18] (An insider-partial approach involves intermediaries from within the conflict setting who as individuals enjoy the trust and confidence of one side in the conflict but who as a team provide balance and equity in their mediating work.) As a member of the conciliation team, I experienced how "partiality" is not always a detriment to intermediary work, and can in fact be a significant resource. The insider-partial approach we saw in operation in the Sandinista-Yatama conflict involved "insider" intermediaries such as Andy Shogreen, who was from a Creole-Miskito family, had been superintendent of the Moravian Church during the war in the 1980s, and was a close childhood friend of Brooklyn Rivera, the key Miskito leader of Yatama. Gustavo Parajon, by contrast, was from Managua and had been appointed by President Daniel Ortega as the "notable citizen" on the national conciliation commission. The middle-range religious leaders whom the conciliation commission drew on were able to use their personal and institutional networks within the context to create a successful response to the conciliation needs of the regional aspects of the overall national conflict.

A parallel example can be drawn from the National Peace Accord structure that emerged in postapartheid South Africa. In this instance, the rubric of formal negotiations between top-level leaders set in motion a process of transition and sociopolitical transformation that specifically contemplated numerous levels of activity across society. The accord created at least seven major levels of activity, running from a national peace committee through to regional and local committees.[19] It contemplated, for example, jointly operated communication centers to monitor and where possible preempt community violence that was threatening to undermine the peace process.[20] Such an effort was a move toward identifying key people in critical locations who, working through a network, would begin to build an infrastructure capable of sustaining the general progression toward peace. Central to the overall functioning of the peace process was the development of institutional capacities through the training of a broad array of individuals to respond to the volatile period of transition.

What the above approaches suggest is that the middle range holds the potential for helping to establish a relationship- and skill-based infrastructure for sustaining the peacebuilding process. A middle-out approach builds on the idea that middle-range leaders (who are often the heads of, or closely connected to, extensive networks that cut across the lines of conflict) can be cultivated to play an instrumental role in working through the conflicts. Middle-range peacebuilding activities come in varied forms, from efforts directed at changing perceptions and floating new ideas among actors proximate to the policymaking process, to training in conflict resolution skills, to the establishment of teams, networks, and institutions that can play an active conciliation role within the setting.

Level 3: Grassroots Approaches

Grassroots approaches face different challenges from those confronting the top and middle-range levels. First, at this level are massive numbers of people. At best, strategies can be implemented to touch the leadership working at local and community levels, but more often than not these strategies represent points of contact with the masses rather than a comprehensive program for reaching them. Second, many of the people at this level are in a survival mode in which meeting the basic human needs of food, shelter, and safety is a daily struggle. Although unresolved human conflict is a central cause of their suffering, efforts directed at peace and conflict resolution can easily be seen as an unaffordable luxury. Nonetheless, important ideas and practical efforts do emerge at this level. We will consider here an outline of a bottom-up approach to peacebuilding and several concrete examples of programs targeted at the grassroots-level population.

Bottom-up approach. One could argue that virtually all of the recent transitions toward peace—such as those in El Salvador and Ethiopia, as well as the earlier one in the Philippines—were driven largely by the pressure for change that was bubbling up from the grassroots.[21] In fact, at times it seems that exhaustion, rather than innovative planned transformation, is chiefly responsible for ending conflicts.

A concrete case of a bottom-up approach has been clearly delineated in the Somali context. First articulated by the Somali members of the Ergada—a forum of Somali intellectuals for peace created in 1990—the bottom-up perspective was later rearticulated in more detail by international and Somali resource groups convened by the Life and Peace Institute of Uppsala, Sweden, to advise the United Nations in its reconciliation work in Somalia between 1991 and 1993.[22]

The approach was rooted in an assessment of three important features of the situation in Somalia. First, since the fall of President Siad Barre in 1991, the formal, political infrastructure of the country had for all practical purposes disintegrated. Second, in the post-Barre years Somalis had come to rely directly on clan and subclan structures for security and subsistence. Third, Somalis have a rich history of traditional mechanisms for dealing with interclan disputes.

Given this background, efforts to identify national leaders or convene peace conferences relying on common diplomatic devices, such as bringing together key militia leaders, would create a superficial structure unable to sustain itself. Instead, the most promising

STRUCTURE ● ● ● 53

approach would be to develop a process that builds on the traditions of the Somali people.

In brief, the bottom-up approach involved a process of first achieving discussions and agreements to end the fighting at local peace conferences, by bringing together contiguous and interdependent subclans, guided by the elders of each subclan. These conferences not only dealt with issues of immediate concern at local levels, but also served to place responsibility for interclan fighting on the shoulders of local leaders and helped to identify the persons who were considered to be rightful representatives of those clans' concerns. Having achieved this initial agreement, it was then possible to repeat the same process at a higher level with a broader set of clans. Characteristic of these processes were the reliance on elders; lengthy oral deliberations (often lasting months); the creation of a forum or assembly of elders (known in some parts of the region as the *guurti*); and careful negotiation over access to resources and payments for deaths that would reestablish a balance among the clans.

These are basic parameters of the process as it was implemented in Somaliland, the northwestern part of the country, which announced its secession in 1991.[23] The process was initiated with numerous local peace conferences throughout the region and culminated in the Grand Borama Peace Conference, which brought together more than five hundred elders. The Grand Conference lasted for more than six months and succeeded in establishing a framework for peace, the basic structure of which helped to significantly diminish the level of fighting and violence in Somaliland as compared to other parts of Somalia, particularly Mogadishu.

Programmatic peace efforts. A number of other important efforts aimed at promoting peacebuilding at the grassroots level suggest a broader scope of possibilities. These efforts can be divided chronologically according to whether they were launched before or after a formal peace structure had been achieved in a conflict situation.

Two examples of peacebuilding efforts targeted at the grassroots level *before* formal peace and electoral structures were established took place in Mozambique, where initiatives emerged from both the Christian Council of Mozambique (CCM) and the United Nation Children's Fund (UNICEF). The CCM-initiated program,

"Preparing People for Peace," was conceived as a way to open up and deal with conflict and peace issues in the Mozambique setting, with a specific focus on the provincial and district levels.[24]

The CCM program began with a national seminar in summer 1991 that brought together church representatives from all of the provinces; these representatives were then given the responsibility for implementing seminars at local levels. An integrated approach was taken to the content of the seminar discussions, which ranged from topics such as religious perspectives on war and peace, to family and church involvement in conflict resolution, to issues of youth, displaced persons and their return, land reform, public health, human rights, and the impact of violence and war on children. On average, each seminar involved between thirty and fifty participants, both pastors and laypersons, and lasted for two weeks. Over the course of sixteen months (toward the end of which the national peace accord was signed), more than seven hundred people participated in the seminars, several of which were held in refugee camps in neighboring Zimbabwe.

The second example from Mozambique was the UNICEF project, "Circus of Peace."[25] The aim in this case was to deal innovatively with the conflict, violence, and militarization facing local communities, especially their youth. Like a circus, the project was organized as a traveling show that wove drama and the arts into its explorations of the nature and challenges of war and conflict and the possibilities of reconciliation, including the skills of resolving conflict. The show not only captivated audiences but also served as a way to publicly grieve over the losses the country had suffered, to address concerns of the people, and to set the stage for changes and movement toward peace.

A third example from Africa is the ongoing efforts of the Christian Health Association of Liberia, which has integrated conflict resolution approaches within broader community and public health programs for dealing with postwar trauma.[26] Conflict resolution components have included training in dealing with community conflict and violence, and in reducing prejudice and enhancing community decision making. The workshops have been conducted in locations around the country as part of the health-delivery system, and have drawn on resource teams made up of conflict resolution trainers, public health officials, and psychiatrists or counselors.

What stands out in all three of these examples is the effort to provide an opportunity for grassroots leaders and others to work at the community or village level on issues of peace and conflict resolution. Programs such as these frequently work through existing networks, such as churches or health associations. These grassroots-level programs are also characterized by their attempts to deal with the enormous trauma that the war has produced, especially among the youth. War at this level is experienced with great immediacy, both in terms of violence and trauma endured and insofar as people live in close proximity and continued interdependency with those who were once, and may still be, perceived as enemies. This is not a matter of political accommodation at the highest level; rather, it involves interdependent relationships in the everyday lives of considerable numbers of people. From personal experience I can attest to the fact that the process of advancing political negotiation at polished tables in elite hotels, while very difficult and complex in its own right, is both a more formal and a more superficial process than the experience of reconciliation in which former enemies are brought together at the village level.

FROM ISSUES TO SYSTEMS

Having used one set of lenses to focus on the actors and appropriate peacebuilding activities to be found at the different levels in a population affected by conflict, we can now employ a second set of lenses to focus on the structural component of an analytical framework for conflict transformation. As we do so, we need to take into consideration both the immediate, "micro-issues" in the conflict and the broader, more systemic concerns. The work of peace researcher and theorist Maire Dugan is of help to us in this regard.[27] Dugan has developed what she calls a "nested paradigm" as a mechanism for considering both the narrower and the broader aspects of conflict resolution and peacebuilding (see figure 3).

This paradigm was developed, Dugan explains, in an effort to explain how the approach of a conflict resolution practitioner to a

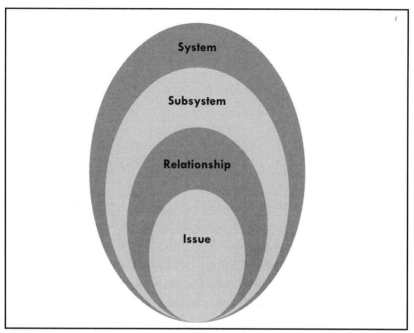

Figure 3. The Nested Paradigm of Conflict Foci.
Source: Maire Dugan, "A Nested Theory of Conflict," *Women in Leadership* 1, no. 1 (summer 1996).

given situation differs from that of a peace researcher. She took, as a practical example, a violent conflict that had emerged in a local school between African American and white gangs of young boys. She speculated that a conflict resolution practitioner, such as a mediator, would see this as an issue in dispute, a case to be explored and resolved between the boys who had been fighting. The answer to the problem, then, would be to resolve the issue that sparked the fight.

Taking it one step further, she suggested that in some instances, depending on the model of practice used, the mediator might see this as not only a particular issue to be resolved but also a relationship that needed to be addressed. In this case, the issue would be embedded within a relationship that needed to be reconciled. Here, the practitioner might move to incorporate, for example, prejudice-reduction or bias-awareness work with the boys in order to increase their understanding of one another and promote reconciliation in a deeper sense. The problem in this instance would be defined as a broken relationship that needed to be restored as part of the solution.

A peace researcher, on the other hand, might see the school fight in the context of a society built on racial inequality and economic inequity. In other words, the boys' struggle might be seen as symptomatic of broader societal structures and systems. The problem might thus be defined as racism. The solution, according to the peace researcher, would be to change society and the social structures that create and perpetuate racism.

In the conflict resolution approach, the practitioner's efforts would be likely to help defuse the immediate face-to-face tensions, and in some cases would also repair the broken relationships. This approach, however, would do little to redress the inequities in the broader system that were at the root of the racial tensions. The peace research approach, on the other hand, would move to label the problem as racism, which would help focus attention on the deeper structural and systemic concerns. But this prescription would offer few handles for dealing with the immediate crisis and the problems of relationship.

Dugan, therefore, adds a third, intermediate level—the subsystem. Here the focus would be on the immediate system within which the boys are located, in this case the school. At this level, a peacebuilding strategy could be designed that would address both the systemic concerns and the problematic issues and relationships. It might involve the development of a schoolwide program that would address the social issue of racism in the context of the relationships in that subsystem. The school, for example, might introduce into its curriculum a required course on diversity and race relations or might host a weeklong training program on prejudice reduction for students and teachers. By such means, the school could bring to the surface and address systemic racism while engaging in concrete programmatic activity that would deal with the immediate issue of gang violence and the need to reconcile the two groups of boys. The subsystem, in other words, is a middle-range *locus* of activity that connects the other levels in the system.

There is an obvious parallel between this systems-level analysis and the foregoing analysis of levels, which related to the actors and peacebuilding approaches found at different levels of a population affected by internal armed conflict. In both frameworks, the middle level provided the strategic link to the other levels.

We can see the value of the nested paradigm by applying it to a specific area of concern within a situation of protracted conflict: the challenge of dealing with roving gangs of armed youth in the streets of Mogadishu, a problem that perplexed people both within and outside Somalia. At the "system" level, this was of course a matter of disarmament and demobilization. An immediate response at the "issue" level might have been to offer the youth money for guns. Closer analysis, however, would reveal such a response to be superficial, one that might in fact exacerbate the situation if the availability of weapons and the socioeconomic reasons that the youth were armed were to go unaddressed.

This is precisely the perspective reached by initial research into the phenomenon of armed gangs in Mogadishu.[28] It was discovered that people there, youth included, were carrying guns for a variety of reasons. Some did so in support of the political objectives of a particular movement. Many people carried weapons to protect themselves and their families. For others, the gun was much more analogous to a job than to a commodity or possession. It represented employment in the form of providing protection—for aid workers or for the delivery of food, for example—or the securing by force of scarce resources and the reselling of the same. Further, at a social-psychological level the gun helped establish and maintain social status—again, not unlike a prestigious job. When gun-toting was seen in this broader systemic context, the offering of money for guns was shown to be comparable to offering cash for a person's job.

The "system" and "issue" perspectives thus raised legitimate but different questions. On the one hand, how should one address the deeper and longer-term issues of limiting the availability of weapons and creating increased security and stability in the setting? On the other hand, how should one meet the immediate challenge of providing an alternative that is roughly equivalent in socioeconomic terms to the status and benefits provided by the gun? Might a subsystem, relationship approach provide a bridge that would link the broader structural concerns and the immediate local needs?

Such an approach was proposed through the Ergada and Life and Peace Institute resource groups. The proposal—aspects of which were explored by the United Nations in Somalia[29]—suggested the creation of a pilot training center. Youth from the gangs in Mogadishu, in exchange for their weapons, would be offered training in various vocations over the course of a year. At the end of the year they would receive the tools necessary for their trade and contracts for employment for a second year. In socioeconomic terms, the plan offered an employment package roughly similar to what the gun could provide. Further, the training context would be structured so as to also provide participants an opportunity to deal with the trauma experienced in the war, interact in a structured environment with their counterparts from other clan militia, and learn basic literacy (the educational system had been totally disrupted by the conflict). In short, the process would create an opportunity for social and economic transformation.

The nested paradigm underscores the need to look consistently at the broader context of systemic issues. It suggests, however, that at the subsystem level we can experiment with various actions that promise to connect "systemic" and immediate "issue" concerns.

At the macro-systemic level, however, we need to create innovative projects that take seriously the major challenges that go beyond the scope of any one internal armed conflict. It seems to me that these should address the production and availability of weapons, the difficulty of creating functional arms embargoes, and the reliance on militarization to provide security. In meeting these challenges, the idea of experimenting in the middle range, or subsystem, offers some guidance and inspiration.

For example, we need to move toward regional arms-transfer control mechanisms, through which countries afflicted by internal conflicts address the issue of arms control within their region. Additionally, disarmament resource groups could be created, made up of specialists from a variety of perspectives, which would generate specific proposals for arms control or demobilization projects in a given region. In this regard one example is the Disarmament Resource Group that was created in 1993 for agencies and groups working in the Horn of Africa. Its mandate is to provide expertise, research, ideas, and support to disarmament, weapons control, and demobilization issues in the region. Its membership—drawn from the United Nations, NGOs, and academia—includes specialists in arms control, peacekeeping, conflict resolution, and humanitarian relief and development.[30] The group has set a research agenda, has performed consultancy and evaluation work for operational agencies, and is engaged in regional arms control advocacy.

CONCLUSION

This chapter has outlined a number of key concepts in the structural side of establishing an overall framework for peacebuilding. We have suggested the need for two basic sets of lenses. One set is used for looking at the overall situation in terms of the levels of actors concerned with peacebuilding in the affected population and the kinds of resources and activities available at each level. The second set provides a means for looking at both the immediate issues in the conflict and the broader systemic concerns. These conceptual approaches have important features in common.

First, both approaches suggest that an integrative, comprehensive analytical framework is not merely instructive but is imperative to meet the needs of peacebuilding today. Constructing a peace process in deeply divided societies and situations of internal armed conflict requires an operative frame of reference that takes into consideration the *legitimacy, uniqueness,* and *interdependency* of the needs and resources of the grassroots, middle range, and top level. The same is true when dealing with specific issues and broader systemic concerns in a conflict. More specifically, an integrative, comprehensive approach points toward the functional need for *recognition, inclusion,* and *coordination* across all levels and activities.

Second, in both of these conceptual approaches, the level with the greatest potential for establishing an *infrastructure* that can sustain the peacebuilding process over the long term appears to be the middle range. The very nature of contemporary, internal, protracted conflicts suggests the need for theories and approaches keyed to the middle range. Although such approaches are informed by deeper systemic analysis, they also provide practical initiatives for addressing immediate issues, and are able to draw on valuable human resources, tap into and take maximum benefit from institutional, cultural, and informal networks that cut across the lines of conflict, and connect the levels of peace activity within the population. These qualities give middle-range actors and subsystem and relationship foci the greatest potential to serve as sources of practical, immediate action *and* to sustain long-term transformation in the setting.

5

PROCESS: THE DYNAMICS AND PROGRESSION OF CONFLICT

● ● ●

Our attention now shifts from lenses for looking at structure to lenses through which we can examine the dynamics and progression of conflict. It has become quite common to talk about a "peace process" as if that denotes a clearly defined set of activities. In reality, the details of and exact procedures for building peace make up a complex, multifaceted endeavor and can vary significantly from setting to setting.

In this chapter I am interested in developing the idea that conflict is a progression and that peacebuilding is a process made up of various functions and roles. Such a perspective suggests the need to situate any given conflict in an expansive rather than a narrow time frame and to look specifically for the elements that make up a sustainable process. We need, therefore, to describe and define more clearly how we understand the progression of a conflict, what we mean by process, the significance and meaning of sustainability in this context, and the relevance of the time frame of operation.

CONFLICT AS PROGRESSION

Conflict is never a static phenomenon. It is expressive, dynamic, and dialectical in nature. Relationally based, conflict is born in the world of human meaning and perception. It is constantly changed by ongoing human interaction, and it continuously changes the very people who give it life and the social environment in which it is born, evolves, and perhaps ends. Those who study social conflict from a scientific point of view and those who wish to find practical ways of dealing with it more constructively are interested in the characteristics of conflict and the patterns that it follows. It is through this exploration that researchers have identified the life cycle or progression of conflict.[1]

In an article that appeared in the late 1980s I suggested that it is useful to look at conflict in terms of its longitudinal progression.[2] The article drew upon a conceptual piece published in 1971 by Quaker conciliator Adam Curle.[3] From his experiences in Africa and Asia where he worked as a mediator, Curle suggested that conflict moves along a continuum from unpeaceful to peaceful relationships. This movement can be charted on a matrix that compares two key elements: the level of power between the parties in conflict and the level of awareness of conflicting interests and needs (see figure 4). The matrix is useful for plotting where in the progression, at any given moment, a conflict is located. As we will see, situating a conflict helps to indicate which potential peacebuilding and conflict resolution functions and activities may be appropriate.

Curle proposed that we understand the movement toward peace through the roles that emerge in a typical progression of conflict through four major stages. In Quadrant 1 in his matrix, conflict is latent or "hidden," because people are unaware of the imbalances of power and injustices that affect their lives. At this point, Curle argues, education in the form of *conscientization* is needed. The role of educator in this quadrant is aimed at erasing ignorance and raising awareness as to the nature of the unequal relationships and the need for addressing and restoring equity, as seen, of course, from the view of those experiencing the injustices.

Increased awareness of self, the nature of relationships, and context leads to demands from the weaker party for change. These demands are rarely immediately achieved and more typically are not even heard or taken seriously by those benefiting from the status quo. Hence, the entry of advocates who work with and support those pursuing change. As described in Quadrant 2, the pursuit of change involves some form of *confrontation*. Confrontation brings

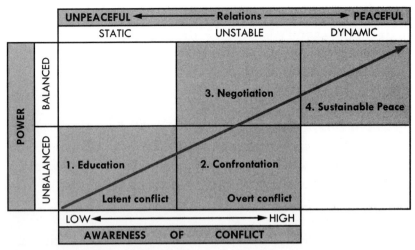

Figure 4. The Progression of Conflict
Source: Adam Curle, *Making Peace* (London: Tavistock Press, 1971).

the conflict to the surface. It is no longer hidden. The confrontation itself, however, involves a series of choices regarding how the conflict will be expressed and how the concerns will be addressed. These choices range between violent or nonviolent mechanisms or a combination of both.

Change will require a rebalancing of power in the relationship by which all those involved recognize one another in new ways. Such recognition will increase the voice and participation of the less powerful in addressing their basic needs and will legitimate their concerns. In Quadrant 3 confrontation moves toward *negotiations* if those involved increase the level of awareness of their interdependence through mutual recognition. In essence, negotiation means that the various people or groups involved recognize they can neither simply impose their will on nor eliminate the other side, but rather must work with one another to achieve their goals. Mutual recognition is a form of power balancing and a prerequisite of negotiation. The roles of conciliation and more formal mediation are aimed principally at helping to establish and support the movement from violent confrontation toward negotiation.

In Quadrant 4 successful negotiations and mediation lead to a restructuring of the relationship that deals with the fundamental substantive and procedural concerns of those involved. This is what Curle refers to as "increased justice" or "more peaceful relations." He is quick to point out that at any point in the progression, conflict can jump ahead, or cycle between several of the quadrants for extensive periods of time. For example, negotiations do not always (in fact may rarely) lead to restructured relationships. Confrontation does not automatically end in negotiation. In fact, the data we considered in our first section suggest that intermediate and war levels of conflict continue virtually unchanged in the confrontational quadrant, with high levels of violence persisting for long periods.

Nevertheless, for our purposes, the matrix provides a useful visualization of the progression of conflict. It is descriptive of how conflict changes and moves over time. The matrix is also suggestive of the multiplicity of roles and activities that might be played to encourage the movement of conflict toward a peaceful end.

PEACEBUILDING AS PROCESS

Much of the public interest in and media coverage of peacemaking centers on the personality of the peacemaker, rather than on what is needed to sustain a constructive process. This is especially true of high-level mediation efforts in which prominent figures emerge and are followed closely as they engage the parties in efforts to bring about negotiations and an end to the fighting.

In contrast to this focus on personality, a number of researchers and practitioners have argued that peacebuilding, and more specifically intermediary work, should be understood as a *process* made up of roles and functions rather than as an activity that resides in the person of the mediator or intermediary team. James Laue and Gerald Cormick initiated this line of thinking in their delineation of conflict intervention roles that includes activists and advocates, as well as mediators and enforcers.[4] More recently, Christopher Mitchell expanded this by developing a broader typology of "roles and functions" of external peacemakers.[5] Table 1 presents his list of thirteen intermediary roles with their corresponding functions.[6] In a similar vein, Louis Kriesberg has suggested a series of intermediary "activities" that are performed by different people at different times in the development of an overall peace process.[7] Finally, Loraleigh Keashley and Ronald Fisher submit that intermediary work can be conceived of as strategies that are matched to different stages of escalation and deescalation of the conflict. Their fundamental point is that different strategies are needed at different stages of conflict development.[8]

My own experience in international conciliation work certainly supports this line of thinking. In almost every situation, it has proved unviable to rely on a single individual or team to sustain and broaden the process of constructive conflict transformation in divided societies. In Northern Ireland, for example, the peacebuilding work that I have had the opportunity to encourage has involved and engaged a variety of people working at different levels and focusing on various aspects of the conflict. Brendan McAllister and Joe Campbell from Mediation Network, for instance, have on some occasions undertaken sensitive initiatives to support direct dialogue between high-level leaders, and yet at other times they have worked on the development of local mediation capacities in the most divided and violent neighborhoods or have fostered dialogue between ex-prisoners. Another example would be the efforts of a network such as District Partnerships Boards in developing a framework for peacebuilding, even though the primary focus of the boards' work is to support economic investment in both Catholic and Protestant communities.

Whether they refer to "roles," "functions," "activities," or "strategies," all these approaches share a view of conflict as a dynamic process and peacebuilding as a multiplicity of interdependent elements and actions that contribute to the constructive transformation of the conflict. Mitchell, indeed, concludes that the overall complexity of an intermediary process is such that to be effective it cannot rely on a single entity. He writes persuasively that

> our concept of mediation might be increased if we treated it as a complex process, to which many entities might contribute, simultaneously or consecutively, rather than as the behavior of a single, intermediary actor.[9]

Table 1. Intermediary Roles and Functions

Intermediary Role	Task and Functions
Explorer (forerunner, reassurer)	Reassures adversaries that other side is not wholly bent on "victory." Sketches out range of possible alternative solutions.
Convener (initiator, advocate)	Initiates peacemaking process by calling for truce, discussions, etc. Acts to enable parties to take part in discussions. Convinces adversaries of possibility of mutually satisfactory solutions and of utility of intermediary process. Provides venue, logistical support, and legitimizing presence at any discussions. May act as facilitator.
Decoupler (disengager)	Assists external patrons to withdraw from core conflict in which they have become involved. Enlists external patrons to fulfill reassuring, endorsing, or enhancing functions.
Unifier (aggregator, consolidator)	Repairs intraparty divisions so that all factions can agree on interests, values, and acceptable solutions.
Enskiller (empowerer)	Develops or equalizes skills and competencies needed to enable parties to reach a mutually acceptable and sustainable solution.
Envisioner (fact finder)	Provides new data, ideas, theories, and options for adversaries to select or adapt. Develops fresh thinking on range of possible options or outcomes that might lead to a solution.
Guarantor	Ensures that adversaries will not suffer overwhelming costs from entering intermediary process. Provides insurance against possible breakdown of process. Guarantees any settlement.
Facilitator (moderator)	Fulfills range of functions during proximity or face-to-face talks between adversaries (e.g., chairing meetings, interpreting positions and responses, etc.)

Legitimizer (endorser)	Helps adversaries accept process and outcome (internally and externally) by adding own prestige to procedure.
Enhancer (developer)	Provides additional resources to assist adversaries reach a positive-sum solution.
Monitor (verifier)	Reassures adversaries about the carrying out of agreement terms in full by the other party or about reasons for nonfulfillment.
Enforcer (implementer)	Polices postagreement behavior by adversaries and imposes sanctions for nonperformance of agreed terms of settlement.
Reconciler	Undertakes long-term actions to alter negative attitudes, stereotypes, and images held at large within adversaries. Builds new relationships across remaining divisions.

Source: Christopher Mitchell, "The Process and Stages of Mediation: The Sudanese Cases," in David R. Smock, ed., *Making War and Waging Peace* (Washington, D.C.: United States Institute of Peace Press, 1993), 147.

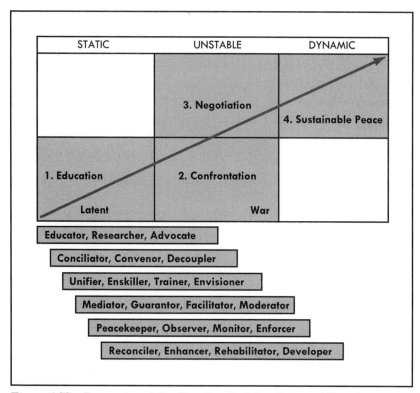

Figure 5. The Progression of Conflict: Peacebuilding Roles and Functions.
Source: Adam Curle, *Making Peace* (London: Tavistock Press, 1971).

Understanding peacebuilding as a process made up of multiple functions, roles, and activities corresponds directly with the view of conflict as progression.

We can return to the Curle matrix presented earlier and add the broad spectrum of roles and functions suggested by Mitchell at their corresponding place in the process (see figure 5). Such a picture helps us visualize peacebuilding-as-process, based on conflict-as-progression. This conceptualization envisions the various roles, functions, and activities as components that together create the possibility of sustainable transformation, moving the conflict dynamic toward the goal of more peaceful relations.

CONCLUSION

In terms of our overall conceptual design, this chapter has proposed a model for understanding peacebuilding as a dynamic process built on two central concepts. First, it was suggested that conflict be understood analytically as a progression that moves through different stages. Second, peacebuilding has been presented as a process made up of a multiplicity of interdependent roles, functions, and activities. In this view, the goal of peacebuilding is to create and sustain transformation and the movement toward restructured relationships.

The Curle matrix provides us with important points of reference in terms of our conceptual framework. First, understanding conflict-as-progression reinforces the idea that peacebuilding involves much more than the achievement of a cease-fire or the conduct of negotiations. Second, the matrix gives us a framework with which to locate the multiplicity of peacebuilding activities within the broader progression of conflict. Preventive diplomacy, for example, could be located at the interface of education and confrontation, where the challenge is to find a way to move the confrontation from violent to nonviolent—and preferably negotiated—modalities. Third, this more comprehensive overview of conflict encourages us to think about how any given activity and role is related to the long-term goal of sustaining a dynamic and constructive process. Linking immediate activities with longer-term goals and developing a framework that helps recognize the interdependence of functions and roles is the subject to which we now turn our attention.

6

AN INTEGRATED FRAMEWORK FOR PEACEBUILDING

● ● ●

Our challenge in this chapter is to outline a framework that brings together the various components of peacebuilding described thus far in a way that is responsive to the realities of contemporary conflict.

In terms of the conflict progression matrix (see figure 5, page 70), many contemporary situations seem locked in a vicious cycle of confrontation and negotiation, where sporadic rounds of talks collapse, restart, and collapse again. In the process, high levels of violence continue to produce humanitarian crises of monumental proportions, as we have witnessed in Somalia, Liberia, Angola, and Bosnia in the first half of the 1990s. When these crises are then captured by television cameras, it seems to sear the conscience of the international community, and pressure mounts to do something urgently. As Ernie Regehr points out, the rule of thumb seems to be that "foreign problems not in the headlines should be ignored, but once they have the attention of CNN they should have been addressed yesterday."[1]

The net effect is the loss of the long-term view of the situation, a myopic focus on crisis negotiation, and a failure to appreciate the multiplicity and interdependence of peacebuilding roles and activities. Too little attention is paid to the prevention of conflicts in the latent stages, particularly at the critical transformative period of movement toward armed confrontation. Once the situation has reached the proportions of a humanitarian disaster, the international community tends to shift toward a crisis mentality that is driven by a disaster-management frame of reference. Disaster management focuses on finding a quick political solution, often in the form of intense negotiations and peace accords, but little preparation is made for sustaining the peace process over the medium and long term.

If we want to create a more comprehensive and sustainable process, we must accomplish two things. First, we will need to reconceptualize our *time frames* for planning and action. Second, we will need to *link* the various aspects and dimensions of peacebuilding. We start with the perspective on time.

RETHINKING TIME FRAMES

As peacebuilders, we have yet to adequately address the nature of our conceptual and operative frameworks in terms of the time frames they represent. For example, in settings of complex emergencies produced by protracted conflict we know that crisis management responses to the humanitarian plight and political reconciliation are linked. What we do not as readily recognize is that they operate within distinctly different time frames. The long view of conflict as progression underscores the importance of recognizing the distinction between the time frame necessary for responding to humanitarian disasters and one that is adequate for the multiple tasks of building peace.[2] It also underscores the relationship between the many forms of crisis-response and peacebuilding activities: Not one is conducted in a vacuum and each has the potential to move the conflict progression forward constructively or to contribute to a stagnating cycle of confrontation. Let us consider this in more detail.

The management of a humanitarian disaster in any situation of war is governed by a crisis framework calling for quick actions that will be evaluated according to their capacity to address the immediate survival needs of the affected population. Yet, while understood in these immediate terms, disaster responses also include planning aimed at making the transition eventually toward rehabilitation and development. The language employed within the NGO relief and development community is reflective of these anticipated shifts.

Thus we talk conceptually about the transition from emergency disaster response to relief operations and to rehabilitation, reconstruction, and development. Central to this framework is the idea that any given immediate intervention is connected to movement toward a longer-term goal, perhaps best articulated as the concept of sustainable development.[3]

This general approach has a clear parallel to the idea of working with the long-term progression of conflict and building toward peace. Both support the idea that the alleviation of immediate suffering must be built upon the concept of transformation, underscoring the goal of moving a given population from a condition of extreme vulnerability and dependency to one of self-sufficiency and well-being. Here, we can put forward two key concepts.

First, *transformation* at this initial level represents the change from one status to another. In the more specific terms of conflict progression, transformation is the movement from the latent stage to confrontation to negotiation to dynamic, peaceful relationships.

Second, *sustainability* indicates a concern not only to initiate such movement but also to create a proactive process that is capable of regenerating itself over time—a spiral of peace and development instead of a spiral of violence and destruction.

Combined, the two suggest a critical point of departure that emanates from our discussion of conflict as progression: The process of building peace must rely on and operate within a framework and a time frame defined by sustainable transformation. In practical terms, this necessitates distinguishing between the more immediate needs of crisis-oriented disaster management in a given setting and the longer-term needs of constructively transforming the conflict.

Crisis response tends to involve specific projects with short-term, measurable outcomes. In the interests of transforming the conflict, however, short-term efforts must be measured primarily by their long-term implications. For example, while achieving a cease-fire is an immediate necessity, this goal must not be mistaken for, or replace, the broader framework of peacebuilding activity. Rather, a sustainable transformative approach suggests that the key lies in the *relationship* of the involved parties, with all that term encompasses at the psychological, spiritual, social, economic, political, and military levels.

The transformation approach suggests another nested paradigm, in this case one that relates time frames and types of peacebuilding activities (see figure 6). In this model, the first circle (on the far left) represents the short-term crisis intervention. For those working in humanitarian aid and development agencies, this type of intervention usually takes the form of emergency relief. For those whose focus is dealing with the conflict, crisis intervention often entails trying to halt the violence and achieve a cease-fire. In an increasing number of situations, both kinds of actions are required—as reflected in the growing use of the term "complex emergencies."

Those people and organizations that undertake crisis intervention think in blocks that rarely go beyond several months: How can we alleviate the excruciating suffering? How can we get the sides to agree to a cease-fire that opens up space for negotiations? The focus is often on the achievement of immediate solutions and goals.

In the second circle, which encompasses the short range, we move to a different modality. To respond more effectively to the proliferation of humanitarian crises induced by conflicts, concerned players in the international arena have increasingly sought to better prepare themselves. The "training" agenda has therefore risen in prominence, particularly in the field of conflict resolution. Training in this context responds to the question: What are the approaches and skills needed to better assess and deal with crises resulting from violent internal conflicts? The nested paradigm suggests that crisis responses should be seen as embedded in the need for better preparation for undertaking crisis management, on the one hand, and for building a capacity to deal more constructively with conflicts before they become full-blown crises, on the other hand. Such preparation envisions a time frame of one to two years, within which a broader array of approaches and skills can be developed and criteria for assessment can be incorporated.

In the fourth circle (on the far right of the model) is the longer-term perspective, which is often adopted by people who seek to prevent conflict and to promote a vision of a more peaceful and socially harmonious future. In this time frame, we think in terms of generations. Elise Boulding talked about this as "imaging" the future.[4] She suggested in reference to peace that we need to have an image, a

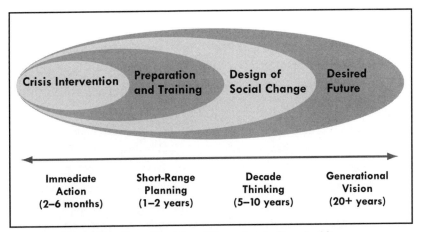

Figure 6. Nested Paradigm: The Time Dimension in Peacebuilding.

vision of what we are trying to achieve in order to build toward and reach that vision. In more specific terms, we need to generate within the conflicted settings the space to envision a commonly shared future. Ironically, perhaps, the conflicting groups in settings of protracted conflict often have more in common in terms of their visions of the future than they do in terms of their shared and violent past. Thinking about the future involves articulating distant but nonetheless desirable structural, systemic, and relationship goals: for instance, sustainable development, self-sufficiency, equitable social structures that meet basic human needs, and respectful, interdependent relationships. The point of this time frame is quite simple: If we do not know where we are going it is difficult to get there. This time frame provides us a horizon for our journey.[5]

Between the immediate and long-term approach we find, once again, the middle-range perspective. In terms of time frame, the middle range thinks in blocks of five to ten years. It is driven by an interest in linking the immediate experience of crisis with a better future in which such crises can be prevented. In other words, the middle-range approach is concerned with the design of social change. This middle-range approach is what a number of conflict resolution practitioners are referring to as "dispute system design."[6] How do we put into place mechanisms that make the transition possible and create a sustainable process that will carry us toward our ultimate goals?

Taken as a whole, the nested paradigm demonstrates that we must respond to immediate crises in a manner that is informed by a longer-term vision. Our capacity to respond to the short-term agenda is more fully developed than is our capacity to take a longer-term view and see distant goals strategically reflected in our short-term action. This is especially important in dealing with protracted conflicts fueled by perceptions dating back generations. As noted in an earlier chapter, one in four current armed conflicts has been under way for more than two decades. I once was nearly thrown out of a conference room in Belfast when I suggested that it will take as long to get out of an armed conflict as it took to get in. While not a literal formula, my suggestion is that we cannot respond with quick fixes to situations of protracted conflict. We must think about the healing of people and the rebuilding of the web of their relationships in terms relative to those that it took to create the hatred and violence that has divided them.

Viewing conflict as a progression provides a set of lenses for rethinking time. It allows us to see not only that humanitarian disasters produced by war require immediate responses that help save lives in the short term, but also that quick fixes in protracted conflict rarely lead to sustainable processes or solutions. More specifically, it suggests that a crisis-driven response to conflict that measures success in terms of arresting disease and starvation and achieving a cease-fire must be embedded within the painstaking tasks of relationship and confidence building, and of the design of and preparation for social change, which ultimately provide a basis for sustaining conflict transformation.

Constructing such a process entails the unfolding of a design "architecture" that moves through stages. The design explicitly envisions short-term crisis responses to protracted internal conflict as embedded in and informed by a long-term point of view. Within the time frame of conflict progression, it is necessary to develop the capacity to think in longer units of time—in decades instead of weeks and months. Such an architecture recognizes and integrates specific roles and functions and their corresponding activities as the dynamic elements that create and sustain the movement along the continuum of constructive transformation over time. What we need are practical mechanisms by which our vision of a desired future can be used to define our response to the crisis; otherwise, the crisis and its dynamics will define the future.

AN INTEGRATED FRAMEWORK

We see here the natural and crucial overlap between the structural and procedural lenses, as elements of a broad peacebuilding paradigm. "Structure" suggests the need to think *comprehensively* about the affected population and *systemically* about the issues. "Process" underscores the necessity of thinking creatively about the *progression* of conflict and the *sustainability* of its transformation by *linking* roles, functions, and activities in an integrated manner. Together, the two sets of lenses suggest an integrated approach to peacebuilding, visualized in figure 7 by linking the two nested models into an overall matrix. The vertical axis is taken from the Dugan nested paradigm that allows us to link the foci and levels of intervention in the conflict. The horizontal axis is the time frame model that links short-term crisis with longer-term perspective for change in the society. The two dimensions intersect at five points, each of which represents a distinct—and all too often discrete—community of thought and action in the broader field of peacebuilding. Let us look at each in more detail.

Root Causes

Those who are concerned with systemic perspectives underlying the crisis tend to pursue a structural analysis of the root causes of the conflict. They often reflect back on the long history of the current crisis to analyze and explain the broader systemic factors that must be taken into account.

Crisis Management

People who have the tasks of responding to the immediate issues and ameliorating humanitarian suffering, who seek a respite in the

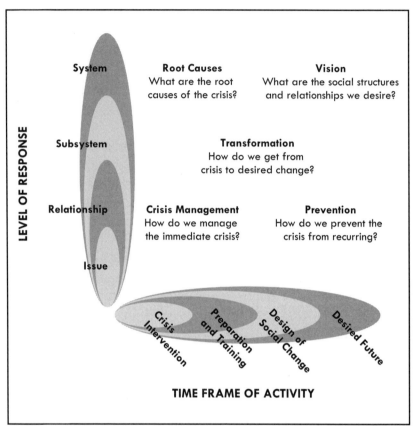

Figure 7. An Integrated Framework for Peacebuilding.

fighting, are most concerned about how to manage the crisis and achieve some agreement between the parties on immediate issues. They rarely have time to review all the information generated by the "root cause" community and are driven by pragmatism and common sense. They want to know what needs to be done and to get it done as soon as possible.

Prevention

At the level of the immediate issues but looking toward the future, another set of people concentrate on how to learn the lessons of the crisis in order to anticipate and prevent its recurrence. Their work involves identifying the factors that precipitated the violence, helping the affected society prepare to better handle such situations in the future, and disseminating to other societies the lessons of what went wrong and what went right.

Vision

With a generational perspective on system-level subjects, another group of people focus on desirable social and political structures and future relationships between those groups currently in conflict. The visions they articulate center on the well-being of coming generations.

Transformation

Where a focus on the subsystem intersects with a concern to think in terms of decades and to design social change, people pose the strategic question, How to move from this crisis to the desired change? Here, transformation is posited at a middle range, which requires input from the other four communities.

The basic proposal put forward in this book is the need for an integrated approach to peacebuilding. Integration begins with a recognition that the middle range holds special potential for transformation, but that change will be needed at every level of human experience and endeavor. Specifically, the middle-range perspective suggests that we need to achieve integration in at least three strategic ways.

- We must develop the capacity to think about the design of social change in time-units of decades, in order to link crisis management and long-term, future-oriented time frames.
- We must understand crisis issues as connected to systemic roots and develop approaches that explicitly anchor issues within a set of relationships and subsystems.
- We must recognize the integrative potential of middle-range leaders, who by their locus within the affected population may be able to cultivate relationships and pursue the design of social change at a subsystem level, thus helping to make the vertical and horizontal connections necessary to sustain a process of desired change.

Here, we can begin to define an understanding of *conflict transformation* that goes beyond the resolution of issues. In essence, conflict transformation refers to change that can be understood in two fundamental ways—descriptively and prescriptively—across four dimensions—personal, relational, structural, and cultural.

Descriptively speaking, transformation refers to the empirical impact of conflict—in other words, to the effects that social conflict produces. In this case, we use the word "transformation" to describe the general changes social conflict creates and the patterns it typically follows. At a *prescriptive* level, transformation implies deliberate intervention to effect change. In this instance, transformation refers to the goals we have as intervenors as we work with conflict.

At both descriptive and prescriptive levels, transformation is operative across four interdependent dimensions. The *personal* dimension refers to the changes effected in, and desired for, the individual. This involves emotional, perceptual, and spiritual aspects of conflict. From a descriptive perspective, transformation suggests that individuals are affected by conflict both negatively and positively—for example, in terms of their physical well-being, self-esteem, emotional stability, capacity to perceive accurately, and spiritual integrity. Prescriptively, transformation represents deliberate intervention to minimize the destructive effects of social conflict and maximize its potentialities for personal growth at physical, emotional, and spiritual levels.

The *relational* dimension depicts the changes effected in, and desired for, the relationship. Here we take into consideration the areas of relational affectivity and interdependence, and the expressive, communicative, and interactive aspects of conflict. Descriptively, transformation refers to the effects of conflict on relational patterns of communication and interaction. It looks beyond the tension around visible issues to the underlying changes produced by conflict in the patterns of how people perceive themselves, one another, and the conflict itself, and in their hopes for their future relationship: how close or distant, how interdependent, how reactive or proactive a role to play, what the other party will want. Prescriptively, transformation represents intentional intervention that minimizes poorly functioning communication and maximizes mutual understanding, and that brings to the surface the relational fears, hopes, and goals of the people involved in terms of affectivity and interdependence.

The *structural* dimension highlights the underlying causes of conflict and the patterns and changes it brings about in social structures. At times understood as the "content" or "substance" of a conflict, the structural dimension may encompass issues such as basic human needs, access to resources, and institutional patterns of decision making. Transformation at the descriptive level refers to the analysis of social conditions that give rise to conflict and the way that conflict effects change in existing decision-making structures and patterns. At a prescriptive level, transformation represents deliberate intervention to provide insight into underlying causes and social conditions that create and foster violent expressions of conflict, and to openly promote nonviolent mechanisms that reduce adversariness, minimize and ultimately eliminate violence, and foster structures that meet basic human needs (substantive justice) and maximize participation of people in decisions that affect them (procedural justice).

The *cultural* dimension refers to the changes produced by conflict in the cultural patterns of a group, and to the ways that culture affects the development and handling of conflict. At a descriptive level, transformation is interested in how conflict affects and changes the cultural patterns of a group, and how those accumulated and shared patterns affect the way people in that setting understand and respond to conflict. Prescriptively, transformation seeks to understand the cultural patterns that contribute to the rise of violent expressions of conflict, and to identify, promote, and build on the resources and mechanisms within a cultural setting for constructively responding to and handling conflict.

In summary, conflict transformation represents a comprehensive set of lenses for describing how conflict emerges from, evolves within, and brings about changes in the personal, relational, structural, and cultural dimensions, and for developing creative responses that promote peaceful change within those dimensions through nonviolent mechanisms. As such, the integrated framework provides a platform for understanding and responding to conflict and devel-

oping peacebuilding initiatives. The overall process of conflict transformation is related to our broader theme of reconciliation inasmuch
as it is oriented toward changing the nature of relationships at every
level of human interaction and experience.

CONCLUSION

When we combine the elements in the integrated framework we
begin to establish an infrastructure for sustaining the dynamic transformation of conflict and the construction of peace. An infrastructure for peacebuilding should be understood as a *process-structure*,
in the way that quantum theory has proposed. A process-structure
is made up of systems that maintain form over time yet have no
hard rigidity of structure.[7] Good examples of a process-structure
are a glacier or a stream coming down a mountain. These are dynamic
processes, flexible and adaptable, yet at the same time they are also
structures that have form and move in a particular direction.

In more specific terms, a process-structure for peacebuilding
transforms a *war-system* characterized by deeply divided, hostile, and
violent relationships into a *peace-system* characterized by just and interdependent relationships with the capacity to find nonviolent
mechanisms for expressing and handling conflict. The goal is not stasis,
but rather the generation of continuous, dynamic, self-regenerating
processes that maintain form over time and are able to adapt to environmental changes. Such an infrastructure is made up of a web of
people, their relationships and activities, and the social mechanisms
necessary to sustain the change sought. This takes place at all levels
of the society.

An infrastructure for peacebuilding is oriented toward supporting processes of social change generated by the need to move from
stagnant cycles of violence toward a desired and shared vision of
increased interdependence. Such an infrastructure must be rooted
in the conflict setting. It must emerge creatively from the culture
and context, but not be a slave of either. The purpose of the process-
structure is reconciliation that centers on the redefinition and restoration of broken relationships. The integrated framework suggests

that we are not merely interested in "ending" something that is not desired. We are oriented toward the building of relationships that in their totality form new patterns, processes, and structures. Peace-building through the constructive transformation of conflicts is simultaneously a visionary and a context-responsive approach.

7

RESOURCES:
MAKING PEACE POSSIBLE

● ● ●

In this chapter we will outline and explore some ideas about resources for peacebuilding. We face an intriguing dilemma in this regard. It is abundantly clear across our globe, both historically and at present, that the expenditures and resources consumed by war far outpace those allocated for building peace. Without adequate resources, explicit preparation, and commitment over time, peace will remain a distant ideal rather than a practical goal. At the same time, throwing money at problems—in this instance, contemporary internal wars—will not alone resolve them. On the contrary, such action may exacerbate conflicts. We need, therefore, to be clear about what is meant by resources for peacebuilding.

The primary goal with regard to resources is to find ways to support, implement, and sustain the building of an infrastructure for peace over the long term. To achieve this goal I propose that we need an expanded understanding of resources. Specifically, I suggest we approach the question of resources for peace under two broad headings: socioeconomic and sociocultural. The former suggests that resources do, indeed, involve a monetary aspect, but that equally critical is the sociological dimension in the disbursement of funds. The latter suggests that people and their various cultural traditions for building peace are also primary resources.

SOCIOECONOMIC RESOURCES

As we look at the question of economic resources for peace, it is not our purpose here to outline specific proposals, numbers, or budgets. It is, however, useful to explore in more detail the need to think sociologically and strategically about the monetary support for peacebuilding in contemporary conflict. This involves a process of creating ways of thinking about *categories* of action, *responsibilities*, and the *strategic commitment* of funds to maximize prospects for the transformation of conflict toward sustainable peace. Each of these items deserves specific attention.

Creating Categories

Among the primary sociological tasks of socioeconomic resourcing is helping people, organizations, and institutions to comprehend, acquire an appreciation for, and create categories of thinking and action related to peacebuilding and to see these categories as legitimate and valid within all levels of the population and during all phases in the progression of a conflict.

To take a parallel example from information technology: The advent of digital information, with modern computers, facsimile machines, and electronic mail, has changed the nature of communication. The fact that the technology became available, however, did not mean that it was immediately understood, used, or maximized. There was a process whereby the public gained a comprehension of and an appreciation for the capacities of the new technology. Subsequently, new categories of thinking emerged, within which action was channeled to maximize the use of technology for communication.

The same is true in the area of what we might call, for the sake of comparison, the growing field of peacebuilding technology. While we have recognized for quite some time the need to find better ways of preventing and resolving wars, we are only in the early stages of comprehending and acquiring an appreciation for the conceptual and practical possibilities and necessities for accomplishing the task. We are still in the early stages of developing the categories in which to think about and carry out action.

During the Ethiopian famine of the mid-1980s, for example, most of the responses by the public and by intergovernmental and nongovernmental agencies working in relief and development were directed at the level of symptoms. Some years later, at the time of the Somali crisis of 1991–92, many of these same agencies and groups were making far more explicit linkages among the perspectives of conflict resolution, peacebuilding, relief, and development. In other words, NGOs and intergovernmental agencies not only saw the increased necessity of dealing with the underlying conflicts in more specific and direct ways, but also began to create categories of thinking about these needs and of funding that reflected that assessment and learning.

One specific suggestion to be made here is for governments and intergovernmental and nongovernmental agencies to create categories of funding related to conflict transformation and peacebuilding. In addition, NGOs and regional organizations such as the Organization of American States (OAS) or the Organization of African Unity (OAU) need to develop internal expertise and response mechanisms relevant to situations of protracted conflict alongside the expertise they already possess in the areas of relief and development. This has, in fact, begun to happen in a number of instances. The OAU, for example, has outlined and begun to implement a plan of action for improving its peacebuilding capacity on the continent. A number of NGOs such as the Mennonite Central Committee and Quaker Peace and Service have developed service programs and resource personnel in the areas of conciliation and conflict resolution.

Creating Responsibility

A further step in the development of resources for peacebuilding is to generate a widespread sense of shared responsibility for the larger, systemic dimension of contemporary conflict.

At a global level, we must find mechanisms for establishing responsibility and accountability for the linkage between profiting from the sale of weapons and the recurrence of armed conflict. Perhaps some form of tax could be levied on those who produce and sell weapons; the funds raised could be used to help defray the social and material costs of dealing with the use of weapons. An analogy would be the taxation of "vice" products such as tobacco and alcohol. At a very rough estimation based on total 1995 arms sales, a 1 percent "peace-added" tax levied on the sales coming from the top ten arms producer-exporter nations would probably yield sufficient money to fund the entire UN peacekeeping operation around the globe.

At the direct-response level, the NGO community should also understand its responsibility from a larger systemic perspective. This is especially pertinent to the way in which the international community responds to major human catastrophes that owe their existence more to wars and protracted conflicts than to natural disasters, such as has been the case in numerous instances in the Horn of Africa. We must seek to understand better the relationship among the elements comprising the NGO community's response to such situations.

For example, while massive emergency food relief is clearly needed to alleviate human suffering, this does not mean that the aid somehow represents an exclusively humanitarian response within the situation. The aid program is, after all, part of a broader system. Our thinking in the NGO humanitarian community has traditionally been dominated by a "natural disaster understanding" of need and outcome. This view tends to restrict the analysis of relief activities to, at worst, the immediate concerns of effective response and, at best, to a measure of effectiveness that includes a transition toward rehabilitation and development. Either approach, however, is very limited in the case of disasters that are created mainly by human hands. The concept of "latent functions" is helpful in understanding what else is needed.[1]

In a crisis caused by a natural disaster, the foremost need is to launch an immediate and effective response to alleviate suffering and stabilize the situation and population, with a subsequent move toward rehabilitation and reconstruction. These are the intended functions of the relief activity. The latent functions of aid in such a disaster might include the reallocation of resources within the system or the benefits certain industries derive from the crisis, as was the case with rising lumber and construction costs in the wake of 1990's Hurricane Andrew in Florida.

In a crisis driven primarily by unresolved and at times unrelenting social conflict, however, whereas the intended functions remain much the same—immediate alleviation of suffering and stabilization of the situation—the latent functions of relief can develop in complex and unexpected ways. To deliver food effectively, for example, feeding centers might be established, which have the latent functions of centralizing aid and increasing internal migration. But the chain of effects does not stop there. The centralization of resources and migration of vulnerable populations further attracts those who, also living off the scarce resources, seek to benefit from the people's struggle. Aid programs can thus contribute to the mobilization and strengthening of militias. In settings where outside aid is in fact the only available resource, this effect is greatly intensified. In the case of Somalia in the first half of the 1990s, this process promoted an untenable situation in a conflict that, in large part, is rooted in the centralization of authority. Relief efforts for vulnerable populations were concentrated in certain regions. The relief aid was sought after, fought over, and ultimately sustained militias, creating a situation in which the delivery of the aid had to be protected. This led to further centralization of relief efforts and the creation of safe corridors for delivery, which displaced militias into areas previously more or less stable. And so the story went, becoming increasingly difficult to disentangle, like the snake who ate its tail: To protect the hand that will dress the wound, we end up exacerbating the causes of the original injury. In one of the best pieces of research on this subject, Mary Anderson has argued that, at a minimum, we should operate on the basis of being sufficiently aware of the consequences of our aid on local conflicts that we can avoid doing harm and aggravating the conflicts through our otherwise good intentions.[2]

It is incumbent upon NGOs operating in situations of protracted conflict to think through these broader ramifications of their programs. They must develop the tools to undertake broad systemic analysis of both the short- and the long-term implications of humanitarian action in settings of conflict. Such analysis must explore both the intended and the latent functions of the proposed humanitarian work. NGOs must also develop categories of funding and action that relate directly and deliberately to the constructive transformation of the conflict. It would be possible, for example, for NGOs to create a self-tax, whereby a portion of their overall relief effort, say 5 percent, would be designated for conflict resolution and peace-building initiatives in settings where their relief activities are needed because of protracted conflicts and wars.

This example is intended not only to clarify the need for increased funding but also to underscore the concomitant need to recognize and promote responsibility. We need to be aware of the larger systemic picture, create accountability of action, and encourage more specific ways to promote the recognition and viability of peacebuilding efforts.

Creating Strategic Commitment

Strategic commitment is connected to an understanding of the complexity and long-term nature of the peacebuilding enterprise. In light of this, efforts must be made to foster a deeper understanding of the broader evolution of conflict, and associated with that, of the multiple peacebuilding functions and activities that are required to constructively transform the conflict over an extended period.

Judging from my own experience on the ground in many situations of protracted conflict, significant economic support for peacemaking seems to emerge when efforts to defuse a crisis or restore peace become highly visible. More often than not, this occurs when "prenegotiations" attract public attention and appear to be progressing toward formal peace talks and agreements. Funds are much harder to secure when they are intended to finance preventive action taken before the emergence of the crisis or to support the implementation of an agreement once it has been signed. Paradoxically, these two activities—conflict prevention and sustaining reconciliation—are probably the most "cost effective" in terms of keeping down the price of destructive, protracted conflict.

It also seems much easier to generate funds for formal initiatives, especially ones involving top-level actors. Middle-range initiatives, infrastructure building, and grassroots projects do not typically attract significant funding, even though the middle range may hold the most potential for building a long-term process and developing a broader peace constituency able to sustain conflict transformation.

Finally, it would seem that far more money is available for supporting the preparation and logistics of military peacekeeping options, despite the fact that such operations have no inherent capacity for building peace. Though still difficult to design, implement, and evaluate, the approaches that are likely to have the most enduring positive impact are those oriented toward relationship building and reconciliation. Yet, these seem to be the least understood, developed, and funded.

The guiding principle for the allocation of funds should be that resources are applied in a strategic manner to effect the maximum constructive change in protracted conflicts. Acceptance of this principle would entail acceptance of a long-term frame of reference; would foster an awareness of how funds can be employed as a proactive investment, and not just for reactive crisis management; and would promote an appreciation for those components of peacebuilding that have the capacity to create understanding and reconcile antagonists.

In sum, the provision of resources for transforming protracted conflict is not just a matter of giving money. It involves creating new ways of thinking about the categories of activity and how they relate to the overall situation. It is about creating a sense of responsibility and accountability for the full implications of actions. And it is about strategic commitment to maximize the proactive elements of peacebuilding.

SOCIOCULTURAL RESOURCES

Our focus now turns to another kind of resource: people and culture. Given the images, dynamics, and consequences of contemporary conflict, it is too often assumed that these desperate situations are devoid of resources for building peace. This assumption is perhaps encouraged by the limited points of contact most of us have with these settings. The media provide us with stories focused almost exclusively on hatred, warmaking, and devastation. We see images of emaciated, vulnerable populations that need food and basic health services. Our only direct contact may be through an influx to our shores of refugees who have lost their homes and livelihoods. The general tendency is to think of peacebuilding as being initiated with outside resources, whether money or personnel. But the inverse is probably true. The greatest resource for sustaining peace in the long term is always rooted in the local people and their culture.

Building a Peace Constituency

An important task in the development of a framework for sustaining reconciliation is to build a peace constituency within the setting. Conceptually, at a very basic level this means that the international community must see people in the setting as *resources*, not *recipients*. In other words, citizen-based peacemaking must be seen as instrumental and integral, not peripheral, to sustaining change.

This point both underscores and is underscored by our suggestion that, strategically, the key to a sustainable peacebuilding framework in contemporary conflicts is the middle range. Middle-range actors are positioned such that they are connected to, and often have the trust of, both top-level and grassroots actors. They have more flexibility of thought and movement than top-level leaders, and are far less vulnerable in terms of daily survival than those at the grassroots. For middle-range actors to develop as the core of a peace constituency, however, three things have to happen

First, it is critical to identify and work with people who envision themselves as playing the role of peacemakers within the conflict setting. I have not experienced any situation of conflict, no matter how protracted or severe, from Central America to the Philippines to the Horn of Africa, where there have not been people who had a vision for peace, emerging often from their own experience of pain. Far too often, however, these same people are overlooked and disempowered either because they do not represent "official" power, whether on the side of government or the various militias, or because they are written off as biased and too personally affected by the conflict.

Second, it must be recognized that the capacity of middle-range actors to find a voice often depends on building bridges to like-minded individuals across the lines of conflict. This is no easy task, but it can be facilitated by external support and initiative. Still, it should be remembered that middle-range actors, not external players, are best equipped to sustain conflict transformation.

Third, the recognition by the international community of these persons as valid and pivotal actors for peace is necessary to legitimate the space they need to develop their potential.

To the degree that middle-range actors capture a vision for their role as peacemakers, to the degree they are able to build bridges to their counterparts across the lines of the conflict, and to the degree they are empowered as legitimate actors by the international community, they and their networks, their understandings of the sensibilities and nuances of the setting, and their immediate and ongoing accessibility to key players and processes become ever more valuable resources for sustaining change toward reconciliation. It is through them that an effective peace constituency can emerge.

Building on Cultural Resources

Consistent with the need to develop and support a peace constituency is the need to build on the cultural and contextual resources for peace and conflict resolution present within the setting. To accomplish this requires, among other things, that we in the international community adopt a new mind-set—that we move beyond a simple prescription of answers and modalities for dealing with conflict that come from outside the setting and focus at least as much attention on discovering and empowering the resources, modalities, and mechanisms for building peace that exist within the context.[3]

Many examples of these resources could be cited. From Somalia we have the extraordinary example of women functioning as forerunners in rebuilding interclan communication, which prepared the way for clan conferences—guided by elders and massaged by poets—that led to local and regional peace agreements.[4] From Mozambique is the aforementioned example of the UNICEF-funded "Circus of Peace," built on traditional arts, music, and drama, which targeted and incorporated children at the village level in conflict resolution and peacebuilding activities.[5]

As a way of exploring in greater depth the use of culture as a resource, we can consider the models and learning about peacemaking that emerge from a Central American context. Over an extended period of involvement in the region, I have discovered that many

Central Americans think about conflict resolution in everyday settings according to three key concepts: *confianza*, *cuello*, and *coyuntura*.[6]

In brief, *confianza* is "trust" or "confidence." It refers to people whom I know and rely on, who "inspire my confidence" and in whom "I can deposit my trust." *Confianza* is based on firsthand knowledge of the person and increases over time. It assures sincerity, reliability, and support. The keys to *confianza* are relationship and time.

Cuello literally means neck, the connection of head and heart, but is one of many vernacular metaphors in Spanish for "connections" that help get things done. In other words, *cuello* is the strategic use of my network. When faced with everyday problems and conflicts, Central Americans are more likely to think first of "who" than of "what" in order to "get out of the problem."

Coyuntura is often translated as "juncture" and/or "timing," but it really represents a metaphor for placing oneself in the stream of time and space and determining at any given moment what things mean and therefore what should be done. *Coyuntura* is "timing" to the degree that timing contemplates the fluidity and art of the possible. In practical conflict resolution terms, it means being present and available on an ongoing basis.

Conflict resolution hinges on these concepts. When experiencing a conflict, Central Americans conceptualize solutions in terms of network resources. They seek help from someone they trust who has the *confianza* of the other side. This is *confianza-cuello*, or what I have referred to as an "insider-partial" as opposed to an "outsider-neutral" modality of third-party assistance.[7] We can note several important characteristics about these cultural concepts and modalities.

First, these natural helpers, or mediators, emerge from within the setting. Their knowledge of the context and their relationships with people are seen as a resource, not an obstacle. Second, they are connected on a long-term basis, and are not "in and out" of the setting. Third, they are chosen not for their expertise or profession, but for who they are in the network. Their value lies not in a service to be performed but rather in a relationship in which they are involved. Finally, in Nicaragua, as well as in more recent experiments in Ethiopia and Somalia, a variant on this formulation of partiality as a resource is a situation in which peacemakers as individuals are close to and trusted by one group or side, but as a team provide balance and credibility.

Translated as "Trust," "Networking," and "Timing," *confianza, cuello*, and *coyuntura* are the "TNT" of Central American peacemaking. Trust suggests a relationally based, holistic approach to mediation that develops over time. Networking suggests that peacebuilding is dependent on knowing people and being connected. Timing is the sensitivity to events and the perception of possibilities. Most importantly, all three argue that long-term commitment, relationship building, and consistency are crucial. Together the three concepts understand peace as a process of transformation based on resources from within the conflictive setting that provide connection before and during the conflict, and ultimately help to sustain the peace.

CONCLUSION

In this chapter we have proposed a broad, integrative framework for understanding resources. It is assumed, of course, that resources are necessary to help initiate and sustain a peacebuilding process. However, resources are understood not solely in terms of financial and material support. It was argued, in fact, that the most critical factor in making resources available is the socioeconomic and sociocultural configuration of the approach.

From this perspective, developing appropriate categories for providing funds and establishing mechanisms for responsibility and accountability at a systemic level and on the ground are as important as the funds themselves. This approach is further enhanced when a strategy is developed that helps orient and target funding toward the points of greatest proactive potential for the transformation of conflict toward constructive outcomes.

Finally, resources must be seen as including people and cultural modalities in the setting. A key element in this process is the building of a peace constituency, particularly among middle-range actors in the affected population. In addition, considerable attention must be given to discovering and building on the cultural resources for conflict resolution that exist within the context.

8

COORDINATION:
POINTS OF CONTACT

● ● ●

We have now outlined a number of components of a comprehensive, conceptual framework for building peace. A critical remaining facet is the coordination and connection of these various
elements. We are not concerned here with the establishment of a
master plan developed by a centralized, controlling "peace authority."
In fact, such rigidity and control could well be the demise of the cre-
ativity, breadth, and flexibility needed to promote the comprehensive
approach. What we *are* concerned with here is the conceptual recognition of the validity of each component and the need to find more
explicit points of contact and coordination to maximize each contribution and integrate the uniqueness of each perspective.

To explore this idea further, we can briefly outline a number of
specific ways such coordination might be pursued and provide
examples of how it might operate. Some of the following suggestions have already been tried; others are ideas that have yet to be put
into practice.

- *Develop a peace inventory.* In my experience of working in settings
  of protracted conflict, a significant shortcoming is the absence of
  a wide-ranging inventory of who is doing what kind of peacebuilding activity. This deficiency becomes more sharply defined
  and problematic at points where the conflict reaches crisis proportions and receives extensive media coverage. In worst-case scenarios, the absence of such an inventory can seriously jeopardize

the longer-term, often painstaking efforts at relationship building being conducted at middle-range and grassroots levels, for these may be ignored, bypassed, or even undermined by the rush to achieve short-term results at the higher levels.

Examples do exist of structures and efforts to achieve coordination. The Central American Peace Accord, with its multiple layers moving from the national to grassroots levels, provided the outline for a coordinated structure. The design of the South African National Peace Accord provided specific places and mechanisms for communication and coordination. A unique, long-term example of coordination is the Community Relations Council in Northern Ireland, which serves as both a resource for establishing connections between peacebuilding efforts and an inventory of actions taken at various levels.[1]

It is useful to take stock and identify the activities under way in the setting periodically during the progression of a conflict. This could be done by commissioning research or (more mutually enriching to the groups involved) by convening a conference to provide an opportunity for people to outline their concerns and approaches.

- *Create clearer channels between the top and middle ranges.* Communication between the initiatives taking place at the highest level and those being carried out at the middle range needs to be significantly improved. One way of enhancing communication would be to create more points of contact and communication between the "first" and "second" tracks of diplomacy—in other words, between official and nonofficial initiatives.[2] Another way would be to secure a far more explicit commitment from the top level to legitimate and provide space for the range of activities needed to sustain the transformation of conflict over time.

  In many situations, progress of this kind could be facilitated by the establishment of a coordination committee linked to both top-level and middle-range activities. Such a committee would be particularly valuable in situations where agreements reached at the top level continually collapse because the infrastructure for their implementation does not exist. This would be all the more important in cases where efforts are under way to design a broader, "national" process.

- *Create peace-donor conferences.* In the general area of development and reconstruction, intergovernmental agencies, particularly those of the United Nations, have initiated the practice of "donor conferences" related to specific crisis situations. These major events bring together UN personnel responsible for the broader coordination of humanitarian efforts, the NGO community, and representatives of concerned governments. Such conferences provide an opportunity for participants to learn about new activities, to project needs, and to coordinate efforts.

  Similar conferences might be convened around peacebuilding efforts. Here the goal would be both the coordination in matching resources to needs and the development of conceptual frameworks for targeting funding toward sustaining reconciliation. Such conferencing should be sought not just at the moments of well-publicized crisis but also at strategic moments in earlier stages when prevention is possible and at later stages when long-term change needs to be sustained.

- *Create strategic resource groups.* A critical aspect of a comprehensive peacebuilding approach is to bring broad-based resources to bear on the overall design of the process and on specific dilemmas faced at particular stages in the transformation of the conflict. A number of ways of achieving this can be explored.

  First, it is too often the case that expertise on various aspects of the conflict and peacebuilding is divided into narrow disciplines or perspectives that are isolated from one another. Peacebuilding would greatly benefit from cross-fertilization of ideas and expertise and the bringing together of people working in relief, development, conflict resolution, arms control, diplomacy, and peacekeeping.

  Second, the overall design of a major intervention in a given setting should be reviewed by a resource group made up of researchers, academic experts, and those who will implement specific strategies on the ground. Such an approach was taken by the Life and Peace Institute in support of UN efforts in Somalia in the early 1990s.[3] In this instance, a group made up of historians, anthropologists, peace researchers, conflict resolution practitioners, and former diplomats was convened to meet with UN personnel and review their plans of action, specifically in the area of the national reconciliation process.

Third, expert review would also be valuable in the case of specific "subsystem" projects, such as demobilization, which require action to deal with immediate concerns, but within a broader systemic framework.

- *Link internal and external peacemakers.* A final suggestion is to better coordinate the work of internal peacemakers, their resources and initiatives, with the efforts of external peacemakers. Prominence is usually given to external peace initiatives in settings of protracted conflict, even though there is no evidence that external initiatives have an inherent capacity for sustaining reconciliation. Every effort should be made to place any initiative in the context of its contribution to longer-term needs. It should be incumbent on external peace initiatives, therefore, to provide space for, create links with, and enhance the capacity of internal resources in the building of a peace constituency.

A SOMALI EXAMPLE

Reference has been made earlier in this book to the initiative undertaken by the Life and Peace Institute in Somalia. I participated in some aspects of this initiative and served as an adviser to the overall effort. The project illustrates, in general terms, the practical application of some of the ideas put forward in this chapter and in this book in general.

The Life and Peace Institute (LPI) is an international and ecumenical center for peace research that was founded in 1985 and focuses on activities related to justice, peace, and reconciliation. LPI's Somalia initiative is lodged within the organization's larger Horn of Africa project. Over the years, LPI has conducted research, published essays, and convened conferences around the issues of peace and reconciliation in Somalia. For example, LPI was instrumental in raising funds for the Ergada, a forum of Somalis interested in dialogue and peacemaking efforts, and in establishing a resource group for the

United Nations' political division when the UN special envoy, Ambassador Mohamed Sahnoun, began his work in Somalia.

Its support for the broader UN efforts to build reconciliation in Somalia led LPI to become more directly involved in peacebuilding activities. The primary focus and purpose of its work has been to broaden peace efforts and encourage participation of Somalis in the construction and implementation of reconciliation.[4] As of the time of this writing, LPI has, since 1991, served both as a connecting point between actors involved in peacebuilding at all levels of the Somali population and as a player itself in a wide variety of activities. A general plan of action was outlined in 1993; this "blueprint" presented a strategy to coordinate various levels of activity and promote a broader base for peacebuilding.[5] Table 2 outlines the proposal.

The blueprint suggested that the complexity of the Somali situation called for a multifaceted, comprehensive approach to sustaining efforts to broaden participation in the reconciliation process. Central to such a process was the establishment of a "coordinated reconciliation structure," which would entail the formation of a peace coordinator unit, with regional reconciliation units within the country and an advisory resource group made up of international participants and Somalis.

Sustaining reconciliation as a broad goal was understood to encompass the following specific objectives:

- to help coordinate the peace efforts of Somalis with the work of the United Nations Operation in Somalia (UNOSOM);
- to help establish a functional infrastructure and network to support reconciliation efforts throughout the country;
- to provide expertise and support to various facets of the overall effort; and
- to provide legitimacy and weight to reconciliation efforts, both inside and outside the country, with a special focus on internal Somali efforts at peace.

In sum, the overall effort was aimed at providing a conceptual scheme and concrete plan of action that linked in-country efforts with external resources; enhanced the role of Somali reconciliation efforts, especially elders' conferences; and reinforced the efforts of

Table 2. Blueprint Outline: Reconciliation Infrastructure.

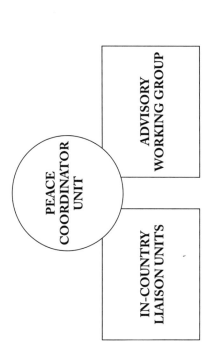

In-Country Liaison Units

1) Establish UN/Somali units placed throughout country:
   a) identify Somali/UN personnel
   b) clarify goals/tasks of units/ three-month blocks

2) Establish clear links with regional *guurtis*/elders

Peace Coordinator Unit

1) Establish core team:
   a) identify and retain prominent figures
   b) clarify role/tasks (e.g., mediation)

2) Establish reconciliation units and advisory working group

Advisory Working Group

1) Establish core consultants

2) Establish advisory group

3) Provide expertise:
   a) think-tank capacity
   b) support for peace coordinator
   c) periodic meetings with in-country units

3) Receive initial training:
   a) team building with units
   b) inputs: conflict resolution, cultural and situational realities, logistics, etc.

4) Support local/regional peace efforts, elders' conferences, women's groups, etc.

3) Establish logistics and communication system:
   a) with reconciliation units
   b) with regional partners
   c) with United Nations

4) Establish in-country/regional offices

5) Establish links to peacekeeping and humanitarian work

6) Establish time frame for key events

4) Provide training:
   a) conflict resolution
   b) translation

5) Provide on-site consulting

6) Provide assessment and evaluation analysis of overall effort

7) Provide interpretation of efforts to international community, NGOs, and governments

Source: Sture Normark, Suzanne Lunden, and John Paul Lederach, "Blueprint: Somali Reconciliation Structure," working paper, Life and Peace Institute, Uppsala, Sweden, 1993.

the United Nations to broaden its peace initiative. Many elements of the blueprint have been implemented, although the changing character of the UN effort and the turnover in top-level UN personnel outmoded certain aspects of the original plan. LPI has supported capacity building for local district councils, numerous women's initiatives, and the broad array of elders' conferences held in Somaliland from 1993 through 1995.[6] LPI has helped provide training in peacebuilding and conflict transformation in various parts of the country and is actively supportive of several ongoing peace initiatives. While at the time of this writing there is still not a functioning government in Mogadishu, LPI efforts have contributed significantly to broadening the peace process and the participation of Somalis at local levels.

CONCLUSION

This chapter has suggested that the major components of a peacebuilding paradigm—structure, process, reconciliation, and resources—need mechanisms that link and coordinate the various facets that each component represents. A proposal has been outlined for creating strategic points of contact and coordination rather than rigid, centralized control. Translating this proposal into practice would involve identifying the diverse initiatives taking place, creating better links between the levels of activities, and orienting the overall process toward enhancing the capacity and strength of internal resources, both with regard to the local peace constituency and in terms of the indigenous cultural modalities for achieving reconciliation.

9

PREPARING FOR PEACEBUILDING

● ● ●

This chapter explores how the peacebuilding framework can be applied in terms of training and preparing people to work in situations of protracted conflict. A guiding question emerges from our inquiry thus far: In what ways does the framework change the way we think about our responses to protracted conflicts? More specifically, how does it change the way we think about preparing for intervention? As presented thus far, the framework poses a set of categories for reflection and planning but does offer prepackaged solutions or recipes for action. Peacebuilding initiatives and solutions, as we have emphasized, must be rooted in the soil where the conflict rages and must be built on contextualized participation of people from that setting if reconciliation is to be sustained. However, we do need to think creatively about those settings and to have available a referent set of categories that help orient our reflection and guide it toward concrete action.

As I have argued elsewhere, much of conflict resolution training has taken too narrow an approach toward preparing people to work with deep-rooted conflict.[1] Considerable emphasis has been put on prescriptive models and techniques for handling conflict, with the result that proposals for action tend to focus mostly on the cognitive skills of analyzing conflict and the communicative skills of negotiation. Proposed intervention strategies are often laden with cultural baggage and rarely engage the trainee as the primary resource in seeking processes and responses appropriate to the conflict setting.

This chapter outlines an alternative approach to training, one which applies the framework for peacebuilding by creating categories for exploration and design while also requiring active participation of the people involved and contextualization of the categories in a given context. This approach requires us to take three steps. First, we must move the conceptual framework into specific and practical categories of inquiry that facilitate a strategic design. Second, we must integrate the categories into a comprehensive whole. And third, we must ensure that the categories lead to ways for taking specific action.

DEVELOPING A STRATEGIC APPROACH TO TRAINING

As a starting point, let me clarify the language and images we use when talking about training. In the field of conflict resolution, we have relied heavily on the word "training" to refer to events and activities in which people are taught specific ways of responding to conflict. It is seen chiefly as a way to pass on to others that which is already known and is assumed to be useful to them in their setting. We have thought less about training as a tool for the design of peacebuilding and responsive intervention in protracted conflict. To regard training in this light, we will need to develop a frame of reference in which we can situate the training activity. A first step toward achieving this is to sharpen our language. I believe it is helpful to talk about training as a process of *strategic capacity and relationship building*. We have here three terms that convey both a purpose and a philosophy.

Capacity building implies that we are oriented toward expanding on what is already in place and available. It reflects an emphasis on the intrinsic value of people's abilities and knowledge, and, at the same time, a recognition that increased insight, learning, and growth is necessary and possible. At a deeper level, the roots of the word "capacity" provide us with an important philosophical orientation. It is built from "capable"—to be able, or to have the power to effect something. In Spanish, *I am able, I can,* and *power* all derive from the word *poder*.[2] The word "capacity," as I would propose to use it here, is linked to a concept of *empowerment*, a term too often misused to cover much and mean little. In my mind, empowerment is related to a fundamental challenge of peacebuilding: How to create and sustain within individuals and communities the movement from "I/we *cannot* effect desired change" to "I/we *can*." From the perspective of our framework, capacity building therefore refers to the process of reinforcing the inherent capabilities and understandings of people related to the challenge of conflict in their context, *and* to a philosophy oriented toward the generation of new, proactive, empowered action for desired change in those settings.

Relationship building suggests that training is not solely concerned with increasing an individual's capacity and skill, but seeks also to develop and build relationships both in and across the lines of the division in the context of protracted conflict.

This has a twofold purpose. At the most obvious level, capacity building in venues where antagonists come together to work and learn begins the long-term process by which these people abandon negative stereotypes and develop a greater understanding of one another as persons. In other words, awareness and realization of increased relational interdependence are intentional goals. At a deeper level, as this chapter explores in greater detail, to make relationship building an intrinsic aspect of preparation is to recognize that most capacity building skills and tools used in peacebuilding and conflict transformation are likely to have a greater strategic impact if they are applied in and by groups and communities. Relationship building responds to the longer-term and coordination requirements needed to sustain peacebuilding in a given setting.

By *strategic* we refer to the need to look beyond the immediate and most visible aspects of a given activity. The word "strategic" should prompt us to ask how the activity impacts the broader setting and whether mechanisms are in place for sustaining the change sought and desired. Conflict resolution training often focuses on preparing people as individuals and pays little attention to their strategic linkages to the setting or to longer-term issues of sustainability. As such, it tends to focus on the event of training as the transfer of content. A transformative approach suggests that training is less about the transfer of content than it is about the creation of a dynamic process involving key people who together focus on the realities of the conflict in their context. Strategic capacity and relationship building require a reframing of training from content to process and from transfer to transformation.

We can visualize this shift in a matrix that I have found useful in the design of training. Figure 8 links two aspects of training. Across the top is an outcome dimension related to the reasons for conducting the training. These are made up of three subcategories that move from general to more specific. At the most general level, we reflect on the *purpose* of the training initiatives within the broader context of the conflict setting. We then move toward decisions about specific activities. At one level, this involves the articulation of the *goals* for a given event; at a more specific level, it involves choices about the *objectives* of activities conducted within the event.

On the left side of the matrix is a time dimension. *Program* refers here to the longer-term contribution of the training; *project* to specific initiatives within the program; and *event* to the actual place and time where people come together for concrete activity. The program is thought about in longer blocks of planning and may well link various project initiatives. The project is thought about as a more discrete, shorter-term block and may link a number of events. The event, however, is a specific and discrete unit of activity, usually conceptualized in blocks of days to weeks. In conflict resolution parlance, if we say "We conducted a training," we usually mean the event itself, which lasted several days or perhaps a week.

The matrix is useful for designing, evaluating, and comparing approaches to training. For example, a pure type of content/transfer approach is depicted by arrow 1. It begins in the event/objective quadrant and ends up in the program/context quadrant. What I wish to visualize with this progression is how the training is conceptualized within, and responds to, the setting. In essence, this approach would be made up of a set of techniques, learning routines, and recipes that create a package that is delivered to the participants; in other writings I have described this as a "prescriptive" approach.[3] It is generally, though not always, assumed that the package meets the needs of the participants and their context. The training is thus event and content driven. It defines the activity according to what is available in the package. The package in turn makes assumptions about what is useful in the context.

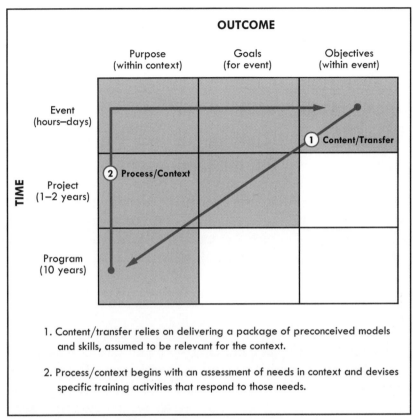

Figure 8. Approaches to Training.

The process/context approach, represented in the matrix by arrow 2, begins in the program/purpose quadrant. It starts with questions related to the nature of the conflict, the longer-term view of change, and the strategic design of training initiatives. In broad strokes, this approach seeks first to understand the needs for change within the conflict system and then designs projects and events that meet those needs. The approach is thus process and context driven. Specific events and the activities that comprise those events are informed by the needs and longer-term view emerging from within the setting and the defined purpose in the context.

By comparing the two approaches we can better visualize how to rethink training as strategic capacity and relationship building. If we seek a strategic and sustainable impact, we must be able to situate the training in such a way that it increases its potential to effect change desired in the setting. According to our peacebuilding framework, this means we must find practical ways to link key people and leaders within the setting, encourage the opening of a space for them to develop a commonly shared vision of a desired future, respond creatively to the immediate and constantly emerging crises, and generate and sustain a dynamic process of change that moves people in the broader context from the crisis to the desired change. In other words, the training must be linked to development of people and their communities in such a way that it facilitates and sustains an infrastructure for peace within their setting.

DEVISING AN INFRASTRUCTURE FOR PEACEBUILDING

The development of an infrastructure for peacebuilding responds to a deceptively simple question: How do we create and support the change from violent crisis to a desired shared future? The idea of an infrastructure rests on a set of key assertions that have emerged in earlier chapters. In settings of protracted violent conflict, peacebuilding requires a proactive change in relationship. Proactive change is possible only if we can sustain efforts to create a vision of a commonly shared future *and* to develop a clear understanding of, and practical responses to, the existing realities and crises. Such change is not an outcome in a static sense. It is, as discussed earlier, a process-structure, focused on the redefinition of relationship at every level of society. To engender and sustain a process of change that moves us from crisis to vision, we need an infrastructure emerging from and adapted to each context where peacebuilding is set in motion.

The elements proposed in the integrated framework (see figure 7, page 80) point toward the qualities and dimensions of this infrastructure. Earlier I referred to this process using the metaphor of building a house. Here I will outline how preparing the architectural design of a house parallels preparing a design for peacebuilding. What we seek is not the solution or the final design. Rather, we want to find the central *categories* of design and inquiry that permit us to move appropriately in a variety of contexts and situations.

Figure 9 presents a working "infrastructure" matrix that outlines four categories of inquiry. In the matrix, each column is built by combining elements from the two dimensions that form the integrated framework presented earlier. Each column in the matrix is integrally linked with the others and cannot be pursued in isolation from the other categories if sustainable processes are to be generated.

The rows across the matrix point out three distinct aspects in developing a more comprehensive approach to peacebuilding. The first poses an initial set of key questions and concerns that are put forward by each column. We can consider the columns as "categories of inquiry" that point us toward a primary point of departure. The second row suggests an initial set of capacities and approaches necessary to answer the questions. The third row provides space for articulating the specific next steps that emerge in response to the questions. This row is left blank, assuming that the movement toward strategy development and specific action must emerge from the context and specific dilemmas, design, and vision that participants in the training would develop. Let us look in greater detail at each column and its respective questions and capacities.

The *crisis* column emerges as we cross-reference the "issue" and "immediate" time frame dimensions from the integrated framework. In this category of inquiry, the focus is on developing a clear understanding of the current realities and parameters faced in the setting, a process that requires the capacity both to engage in conjunctural analysis of the immediate situation and to frame the salient issues therein as dilemmas. The strategic choice facing this column involves the capacity to recognize which of the many issues and problems inherent in a crisis situation are the ones that, if not addressed, will block constructive change. An example may be useful here.

In Northern Ireland, the unilaterally declared cease-fires of 1994 were heralded as a breakthrough on all sides and opened up a period of de-escalated violence and a space for dialogue. However, over the next eighteen months a comprehensive political arrangement at the highest political level could not be reached; top-level negotiators could not agree even on a commonly defined and accepted framework

Figure 9. A Working Matrix for Developing an Infrastructure for Peacebuilding.

REALITY ——→ TRANSFORMATION ——→ DESIRED FUTURE

	CRISIS Issues: 2–6 months	PEOPLE Relationship: 1–2 years	INSTITUTIONS Subsystem/Design: 5–10 years	VISIONS System/Generation: 20+ years
Key Questions and Concerns	• If not addressed, what will block constructive change? • What are the central dilemmas facing peacebuilding in this context? • What are the most pressing immediate needs? • How is immediate intervention linked to midterm goals? • How are top, middle, and grassroots work linked?	• Who has the greatest potential to serve as an agent of change? • Who has respect, linkages, and understanding across levels of conflict and across divisions? • What training/capacity building would enhance their ability to impact the situation? • In this context, what prepares people and communities for reconciliation?	• What key networks and sectors hold potential for conflict transformation and sustaining peace? • What are the likely sources of violent disputes in this setting? • What will be needed to handle those disputes constructively? • What resources exist in the cultural context that shape sociopolitical landscapes? • What are realistic 5–10-year goals for this setting?	• What are the long-term visions for peaceful communities in this setting? • Who are the dreamkeepers in this setting? • What appropriate mechanisms exist for engaging people and institutions in imaging the future? • What systemic changes are needed, internally, regionally, and globally to achieve those visions?

Capacities and Approaches			
• Develop conjunctural analysis capacity. • Develop dilemma analysis and framing capacity. • Develop latent function analysis capacity. • Develop capacity to link official and nonofficial approaches to sustaining negotiations and peacebuilding. • Link relief, development, and peacebuilding initiatives.	• Develop adequate training and capacity building programs (permanent courses). • Develop "vertical/horizontal" analysis capacity for identifying strategic agents of change (middle range). • Develop strategic team building capacity.	• Develop funding capacity for strategic institution building, related to "vertical/horizontal" analysis. • Develop dispute system design capacity. • Develop violence prediction capacity. • Develop holistic response initiatives (internal/external). • Develop cultural resources for peace capacity. • Develop "flex" funds for peace innovation efforts.	• Support and provide space for peace constituency prophets and messengers. • Develop transformative media capacity: poetry, books, storytellers, radio, movies. • Develop capacity for strategic social futures design, imaging the future at community and national levels.
Next Steps/ Necessary Tools Based on the above questions, develop specific ideas, strategies, and steps	1. 2. 3.	1. 2. 3.	1. 2. 3.	1. 2. 3.

for negotiation. At the community level, an "issue" emerged with the potential to affect not only the local communities but also the peace-building system as a whole—namely, the "parading" season of summer 1996 and the resulting sectarian boycotts of local businesses. In this situation, the "issues" and the reactive dynamics they sparked rein-forced the worst fears on both sides, sharply increasing the level of polarization at a time of raised expectations for the proactive move-ment toward redefining the historically antagonistic relationship.

In terms of the *crisis* column parading is an immediate, regularized issue that, if left unaddressed, will continue to block desired change. It is based on a series of dilemmas related to identity that could be posed as follows: How do we create the space for each community to express its historic identity and at the same time increase interde-pendence of relationship, mutual understanding, and respect rather than exclusivity and threat? Framing the issue as a dilemma helps us see two seemingly contradictory energies—distinctive community identity and cross-community interdependence—that must be held together as we think about specific and immediate responses; it also provides a mechanism for measuring how that response relates to the longer-term goal of redefining and rebuilding relationships.

Returning to the matrix in figure 9, the far-right *visions* column represents the intersection of the systemic focus and the generational time frame from the integrated framework. Here, we raise questions about how to create the space for vision to emerge from within the setting. To reiterate, from the perspective of peacebuilding, it is dif-ficult to pursue desired change unless some vision of that change is articulated. Settings that are characterized by high levels of violence and generational trauma, however, are often driven by multiple day-to-day crises, which tend to reduce or eliminate the space for vision development. Those people who try to develop a vision of change are often disdained as "dreamers," idealists with little understanding of the realities on the ground.

However, the inverse is true. To escape the crisis in which they are trapped, people must imagine and articulate the kind of com-munity they desire. They must not envision the future as a final destination that is mechanistically planned, but must instead engage one another, as communities, in the process of looking toward the horizon of reconciliation, toward that place where they can envision living in an interdependent and commonly defined future, even though at this point it is not yet possible.[4] Such reflection informs the decisions and strategies that are pursued in the immediate future inasmuch as it serves as a sounding board for a variety of options present at any given time. This suggests that we need to develop appropriate mechanisms for engaging people and their institutions in imaging their future while still in the midst of crisis. In sum, we need to develop the strategic social capacity to dream and to recognize the role of dreamers.

The middle two columns, *people* and *institutions*, represent the infrastructure for peacebuilding. In essence, they serve as the supportive foundation for sustaining the transformation from the existing reality to redefined relationships in a commonly defined future.

The *people* column focuses on questions about both individuals and their relationships, and on increasing their capacity to respond creatively to the challenges of conflict in their context. On the one hand, the questions are framed to help us think about what is needed to prepare people and their communities for reconciliation. This is forward, rather than purely reactive, thinking. On the other hand, the strategic element comes with the capacity to locate those people who create broader linkages and as such are most able to serve as agents of change within the society. In other words, rather than thinking about capacity and relationship building in a generalized fashion across the setting, we pose here the challenge of locating within the setting those people whose involvement in peacebuilding will serve as a catalyst and then create a critical mass capable of affecting and sustaining change processes across the affected population. This I refer to as a capacity for performing "vertical" and "horizontal" analysis. Returning to our pyramid diagram (see figure 2, page 39) "vertical" represents people and networks that connect the highest with the middle-range and grassroots levels of leadership. "Horizontal" refers to the relationships that cut across the lines of division within the society that form the current expression of the conflict. When we combine these two, we are looking for people who connect both levels of leadership and bridge the divisions. These are considered to be strategic agents of change within the society.

The *institution* column links the design of social change with the subsystem analysis, and suggests that sustainability depends on more than the goodwill of a few well-intentioned people. If it is to be sustainable, peacebuilding must involve a process of social organization that helps create and sustain a new reality. This requires engaging the conflict setting as a system, rather than focusing attention on the determination of the rights and wrongs of the individuals and groups involved in the conflict. Creating a new reality is a process that must be strategically engaged since systemic change is rarely easy to achieve and often poses a challenging paradox in terms of the outcome dynamics: When it is slow and takes place over a long period, the process of change can create a sense of frustration and hopelessness; when it is rapid and uncontrolled, it can produce high levels of violence and volatility. The challenge lies in finding ways to create a process-structure of change that engenders hope despite its slow progress.

In chapter 4 I suggested that by seeking to promote subsystem change, we are able to address the immediate issues while also acting to create a way forward for broader systemic change. In the matrix, the *institution* column orients our thinking toward recognition of the broader patterns of conflict and the emergence of violence in the setting, with a particular focus on the subsystem level. It pushes us to develop the capacity to predict where significant violence will erupt and to design the mechanisms for its prevention and constructive transformation at levels that are accessible to, and that broaden, local participation. In this sense, the infrastructure for peacebuilding combines the elements of preparing strategically located people to build relationships with the engagement of their networks, sectors, and organizations so as to generate accessible and sustainable processes.

The second row in the matrix outlines a series of capacities and approaches that accompany each column. Rather than approaching the challenge of peacebuilding as merely a matter of technique, these capacities point toward a more dynamic understanding of preparation that requires holistic thinking and a firm grounding in the specific context. In this kind of training, participants are seen as resources for generating ideas and strategies rather than as recipients of rote information and models. To a large degree, the various capacities represent organizing categories for facilitating and building on the understanding and knowledge people have of the setting and dynamics of their conflicts. In practical terms, this approach to training suggests the need for people to develop a set of capacities that undergird the design of an infrastructure for peacebuilding. The capacities relate and link three elements: *articulating* a desired future; *understanding* the immediate crisis or situation; and *outlining* a strategic approach that permits movement (transformation) from crisis to desired change. A descriptive list of such capacities could include the following:

- *Conjunctural analysis.* The capacity to identify, understand, and strategically analyze the immediate situation-in-context, with an eye toward locating the social, political, economic, and cultural relationships that may block and/or hold potential for creative transformation of conflicts.
- *Latent function analysis.* The capacity to envision the unexpected (and at times unwanted) consequences and outcomes of program initiatives (relief, development, peacebuilding) in contexts of protracted violent conflict.
- *Dilemma framing.* The capacity to articulate the central dilemmas facing the people on all sides of a conflict, both in terms of immediate impasse and long-term divergent views of the future. Dilemmas are a useful and nonantagonistic mechanism for reframing the specific concerns and issues facing people in a given context in a way that creates an integrated and holistic understanding.
- *Appropriate human capacity building for conflict transformation (training design).* The capacity to recognize the kind of educational tools and skills needed to prepare people to handle and respond to conflicts in their own context. This involves design that is contextualized in terms of content and delivery, and assumes a high degree of local participation and ownership.
- *Training program delivery.* The capacity to conduct workshops, convey ideas, and elicit local participation and knowledge useful for implementing the design developed in specific contexts.

- *Horizontal and vertical analysis.* The capacity to locate critical resource people who are strategically embedded in networks that connect them vertically within the setting (high-level, middle-range, grassroots) and horizontally within the conflict, in terms of their willingness and ability to work with their counterparts across the lines of division within the society.

- *Strategic team building design.* The capacity to identify, encourage, convene, and support peacebuilding teams within the society who have vertical/horizontal capacity. (This approach favors the model of intermediaries as insider-partial teams rather than outsider-neutral experts.)

- *Strategic funding.* The capacity to pinpoint funding in ways that support and encourage the movement toward long-term peace. Strategic funding is less concerned with amounts of money than with quality of focus and centrality of activity to long-term sustainability of the processes to be generated. It includes human, institutional, and project resourcing, as well as "flex" funds that permit quick response, innovation, and experimentation.

- *Violence prediction.* The capacity to analyze situations and predict and project future trends of violence. Such analysis signals possible preventive activities. This is not a "conflict prevention" but rather a "violence prevention" capacity.

- *Dispute system design.* The capacity to envision and develop the human and institutional capacities for handling ongoing conflicts in a setting so that they lead to creative change and interaction rather than to destructive, violent outcomes. It assumes conflict to be a normal human experience in all settings, but attempts to develop appropriate social mechanisms for transforming the conflicts.

- *Contextualized conflict response mechanisms.* The capacity to design and implement specific processes for handling and responding to critical, often violent expressions of conflict.

- *Holistic response design.* The capacity to understand the deeper causes of, and the factors contributing to, protracted violent conflict and to develop response mechanisms oriented toward not only the symptomatic expression of the conflict (for example, negotiations on cease-fires) but also the underlying issues (for instance, weapons flows).

- *Cultural resource analysis.* The capacity to identify cultural resources (and impediments) that contribute to (or obstruct) peacebuilding, providing building blocks for designing appropriate responses and mechanisms within a given setting.
- *Transformative media design.* The capacity to recognize media and communication devices able to impact a broader audience within a setting by providing alternative and accurate news and by presenting a vision of peace through an appropriate cultural form (poetry, movies, popular theater, and so forth).
- *Strategic social futures design.* The capacity to engage people, groups, and societies in articulating and pursuing their visions of a peaceful future.
- *Transitional peacebuilding design.* The capacity to see linkages across time frames and design transitional mechanisms that help people or programs move from crisis to long-term transformation.

Each of these capacities could be described in more detail by inviting people to draw on their knowledge of their own setting. Let us take the third item in our list, dilemma framing, as a case in point. As we approach deep-rooted conflict, we typically see problems that seem insurmountable and that pose outright contradictions as framed by the people involved. For example, when Somalia faced starvation, those of us working in the international relief community felt at times that we were forced to chose between either sending in food and relief aid even though it contributed to the ongoing war, or not sending any food in order to avoid perpetuating the war but thus doing nothing to alleviate the enormous humanitarian plight. Far too often, we framed the situation as presenting either/or choices: *either* we send food and risk war, *or* we support the peace effort and do not send food.

To pose this as a dilemma suggests another way of framing the concerns, energies, and issues in a conflict. Dilemmas and paradoxes offer the possibility that in almost all conflict situations we are dealing not with outright incompatibilities, but with different aspects of an overall situation. These aspects actually represent concerns that function as energies in the conflict system. If we can identify key concerns of the situation and hold them up as systemic interdependent energies and goals, we can better see the situation as a whole rather than getting bogged down in the fragmentation that is represented in the either/or frame of reference. There are two ways to do dilemma framing—a positive and an avoidance formulation.

Positive dilemma formulation frames two energies in conflict as legitimate and necessary to address. It is based on the following formula:

How can we do A and at the same time address B?

How can we deliver food to the starving population
in a way that will encourage the rebuilding of
broken local relationships?

Here, the first energy is a humanitarian concern for delivering food to people who need it. This is a legitimate and necessary task. The second energy seeks to encourage the rebuilding of local relationships that have deteriorated into fighting, violence, and hatred. This is also a legitimate concern. To hold both up at the same time means that we look for options that link these two as interdependent goals. They are different but ultimately linked.

Avoidance dilemma formulation addresses the same energies, but frames at least one of them with the goal of avoiding an undesired outcome. It is based on this formula:

How can we do A and at the same time avoid B?

How can we deliver food to the starving population and
prevent this resource from falling into the hands of local
militia leaders who will use it to buy more weapons?

Here, the first energy is the concern for delivering a resource, food. The second is a concern that this resource not be used to promote the war effort. When we hold the two up together, we again are articulating interdependent goals that help us think more creatively about our options and actions, but in this case we wish to avoid some of the consequences of our actions.

Dilemma framing is a fundamental aspect of peacebuilding. It looks for a framework that sees the bigger picture yet is able to move toward clear understanding and specific action. The basic idea is this: To identify and work with dilemmas is a way to frame the energies in a conflict such that we can more clearly identify our goals and seek innovative options for action that create and link sustainable and specific action. Dilemma analysis is an example of a category of training that involves both a way for organizing our thinking and inquiry *and* the need for specific, contextualized application that builds on the resources brought by the participants. It is less a technique than it is a lens for looking at situations. It requires knowledge about the setting and a new way of thinking. As a training tool, it is process oriented in that it facilitates but does not prescribe action.

TRANSFORMATIVE TRAINING: AN EXAMPLE

Over the past fifteen years, I have been directly involved in the design and delivery of conflict transformation and peacebuilding training courses in more than thirty countries. As reflected in the conceptual framework put forward in this book, the insights gained from these activities have increasingly pushed my thinking in the direction of how to develop training programs that are more contextually relevant and strategically designed to maximize their constructive impact on the protracted conflict. In recent years, in collaboration with colleagues working with peacebuilding resource centers—Justapaz in Columbia and the Nairobi Peace Initiative in Kenya—I have experimented with a more comprehensive and strategic approach to training. This approach has suggested some guiding principles that perhaps are best understood by looking at their application in the Colombian context.

Colombia is by most accounts one of the most violent countries in the world. It has spawned and sustained a guerrilla war with multiple armed groups for more than thirty years, the longest war in the hemisphere. Between thirty-five and forty thousand people are killed each year for reasons that blur the line between crime and war.

Numerous drug cartels are active and have their own standing armies. Violent land conflicts pose a particular threat to the indigenous and Afro-Caribbean communities in various parts of the country. Columbia exemplifies the challenges of protracted conflict at nearly every level of its society.

In this context, a concerted effort has been made over more than a decade by church and community organizations, universities, and various government agencies to find practical and innovative ways to face the realities of violent conflict and build peace. I first worked in Colombia providing conflict resolution seminars in 1988. Shortly thereafter, Justapaz (Just Peace), a resource center for conflict transformation and nonviolence, was established by the Mennonite Church of Colombia. Its mission was to promote nonviolent transformation of conflict, to advocate for human rights, and to provide peace education and conciliation services.

In 1993 Justapaz and the Institute for Peacebuilding at Eastern Mennonite University in Harrisonburg, Virginia, began a process of assessing the needs for training and the modalities by which it could best be delivered and make a strategic impact on the setting. Our perspective suggested that too much of the training to that date had been based on sporadic, one-off events that had sparked interest but had neither created sustained initiative nor dealt adequately with the complexity of the violent conflicts in Colombia. With Ricardo Esquivia, the director of Justapaz, we proposed the design of a *permanent course*. Translated from Spanish, *permanent* refers to the idea of ongoing or continuous, *course* to the notion that this educational effort needed to involve a working and teaching laboratory. Launched in 1994 with support funding from the McKnight Foundation, the permanent course began to bring together people from all sectors of Colombian society.

Our initial effort was designed to provide a regular venue for training and exchange. It was built on two premises. First, there was a need to more explicitly link short-term crisis intervention and intermediate-term conflict transformation training with longer-term institution building across the Colombian setting. As a result, we were interested in working at training with individuals and their respective institutions. We needed to move beyond the concept of "training as a short-term event" and toward the conceptualization of "training as the development of people—and their programs—in context." This involved working with people over an extended period in such a way that they were supported not only by receiving "event-based" input but also by regular communication with others as they attempted to apply and work out the modalities of conflict transformation in their local settings.

We created a venue made up of a series of linked training workshops conducted within a longer-term framework of the course. Originally, we proposed that people who participated in the course—who for the most part were working in programs with social justice and peacebuilding dimensions—commit to regular participation in a program lasting between fifteen and eighteen months. During the course, several intensive workshops would be separated by interim periods in which the participants could apply the course material in their home settings. Each workshop would be built around a theme, but would provide ample space for participants to reflect on their practical work. Since 1994, we have conducted eight of these workshops around themes that varied from broader topics such as "Conflict and Development," "Designing an Infrastructure for Peacebuilding in Colombia," and "Responding to Violence," to more technically oriented workshops on "Conciliation and Interviewing Skills."

Our second premise was that there was a need to think more comprehensively about conflict transformation and peacebuilding as dynamic processes in the Colombian context. This approach inspired us to look beyond the technical side of negotiation and the handling of conflict issues and toward the building and sustaining of social processes and structures. More specifically, we believed that peacebuilding must establish concrete linkages between levels of society, connecting the efforts of higher-level negotiations with midlevel participation and grassroots programs in the establishment of a social infrastructure to sustain long-term social change. This suggested a need to think strategically about *who* might be convened.

Although the workshops were at first oriented primarily toward people involved in the work of community justice centers, the course soon developed into a venue that included a much wider array of levels and applications. For example, in the "Infrastructure for

Peacebuilding" workshop conducted in 1995, more than seventy people participated. They included activists and conciliators from communities in all the major regions of Colombia and from university programs, government ministries, churches, and nongovernmental social agencies. Every day a report was compiled from the materials used and the contents and results of that day's discussions; the report was then e-mailed to five regional centers that were conducting simultaneous workshops. As of the time of this writing, the permanent course is no longer conceived of as a training process with a beginning and an end. Rather, it has become a permanent venue for the development of peacebuilding practitioners in Columbia, and one of the few training programs that links a wide variety of people working at different levels. It has helped to spawn and service a countrywide community justice network and has supported the training of people involved in local conciliation centers.

This approach to training was built on the following principles:

- Understand education as a process of action-reflection, in which people are invited to participate actively in the development and application of peacebuilding strategies and practices.
- Approach training as a process of linked events that provide a venue for reflection by the broader group and for the direct exchange of ideas among workshops.
- Develop the process as a venue for linking "not-like-minded" people and different levels of society, and make the development of ongoing relationships an explicit goal of the training.
- Provide thematic focus for the workshops so that each is immediately relevant to the developing practice of its participants, as identified from their context.
- Approach the overall design of training as a long-term form of intervention in the setting, not primarily as a single event.

CONCLUSION

In this chapter I have proposed a set of ideas for applying the peacebuilding framework in education and training practices. A framework for building peace should, I have suggested, provide avenues for direct, practical action that makes an impact on the overall conflict system. We must approach training in a way that takes into account three needs: to respond to the immediate and constantly emerging crises in the situation; to create a space for the development of a shared vision of a desired future; and to develop an infrastructure that encourages and supports the changes necessary to move from crisis to vision.

Transformative training is conceptualized as an intentional form of response to the conflict system, as an intervention—and not merely as a tool for the education of individuals. To envision training as a transformative component of peacebuilding requires that we create a strategic design in terms of *who* participates and that we create a *process-oriented* design for the content and delivery of the workshops. To pay attention to who participates indicates that we understand that training is a venue for relationship building. To create a process-oriented design shows that we approach training as a strategic component of peacebuilding in the setting that helps link people's knowledge of their own setting with categories of inquiry that facilitate the development of people, their institutions, and the strategic design of responses relevant to their setting.

10

STRATEGIC AND RESPONSIVE
EVALUATION

● ● ●

The purpose of this chapter is offer some initial reflections about the challenges and dilemmas of evaluation in the field of peacebuilding. It is based on a paper I wrote about practical approaches to ongoing evaluation of the OAS initiative in support of the Guatemalan peace accords of 1996.[1] My intention here is provide a way to think about evaluation that emerges from the peacebuilding framework presented in this book.

To evaluate peacebuilding initiatives in societies divided by protracted, violent conflict, we need practical mechanisms that are both *strategic* and *responsive*. Such tools are built using a set of lenses that allow us to see more clearly our goals and vision for the future, and at the same time facilitate practical reflection about the nature of peacebuilding activities. "Strategic" and "responsive" suggest that evaluation, like any other peacebuilding activity, must face the realities of the context and promote desired change in the society that is moving from war to peace. Evaluation, in other words, is not a neutral, external element. It is and should be an intrinsic aspect of peacebuilding.

In this chapter I suggest three elements that provide a way to engage the challenge of strategic and responsive evaluation. First, I outline some of the *dilemmas* facing the funding and evaluation of peacebuilding. Second, I suggest an initial list of *working assumptions* that emerge from the peacebuilding framework and that help establish a common point of departure for looking at evaluation. Third, I provide an exploratory set of suggestions about the kind of *tools* that emerge from the peacebuilding framework and point toward the development of strategic and responsive evaluation.

FUNDING AND EVALUATION: DILEMMAS IN PEACEBUILDING

We are faced with a unique challenge in seeking the resources necessary for initiating and sustaining peacebuilding processes. On the one hand, we have to contend with the fact that the money invested in preparing for war far outstrips the resources invested in explicit preparation for peace. On the other hand, it is also clear that peace processes, particularly the components related to conciliation and mediation, depend more on the development of new relationships, increased interdependence, trust, commitment, and proper timing than they do on dollars. Looking constructively at the funding of peace and the evaluation of what is done on behalf of peace is a complex but necessary challenge. An important starting point is to identify a number of key dilemmas that underlie this challenge.

The Project Dilemma

Most funding agencies, private donors, and government agencies that contribute to a wide variety of peace initiatives have tended to adopt a "project" approach toward evaluation. This approach assumes a kind of packaging of work and activities that lead to proposed outcomes. Projects are seen as discrete, concrete, and measurable units of activity bounded by parameters such as time and completion of tasks. Funds are disbursed to make possible the initiation or completion of the activity. Herein lies both the challenge and dilemma.

Peacebuilding is fundamentally rooted in the building of relationship and trust. I have argued that it involves developing a process-structure, which in turn involves redefining relationships, envisioning how people will work together in interdependent ways, and changing the way people structure and conduct their relationships. These changes take place in settings where events are fluid, emotions are charged, violence has been immediately experienced by many people, and, more often than not, perceptions and misperceptions have accumulated over generations. As such, peacebuilding activities do not always correspond smoothly with the categories of thinking established for relief, development, or other social projects. Building peace is often more about creating space, developing relationship, persevering in spite of overwhelming pessimism, and being flexible enough to respond to emerging opportunities, meager as they may be.

Peacebuilding is about *generating adaptive and dynamic processes.* Some aspects of peacebuilding—for example, training projects and the development of manuals—do fit well within the "project" approach. For the most part, however, and certainly in the case of funding and evaluation, project-oriented thinking may well limit rather than facilitate peacebuilding. The challenge lies in developing new ways to think about funding that correspond to the realities of the work involved.

The Time Dilemma

A related issue is the intersection between peacebuilding and time categories. Most projects are time-bound in ways that measure progress by connecting task and outcome. This is certainly neither unreasonable nor illogical. However, with a process of building peace, particularly in settings of deep-rooted violence, we are faced with a complex set of dynamics and time frames.

First, conflicts are dynamic, not static, processes that emerge from what we might call, to borrow a term from Ed Hall, "polychronic simultaneity": multiple people creating multiple events at the same time.[2] The consequences of polychronic simultaneity are especially unpredictable in settings of protracted conflict. Second, peacebuilding faces the task of linking the long past with the emerging present—or, to borrow a term that originated in Latin America, it is *conjunctural* by its very nature. It must find a way to constructively recognize and take into account the history of the conflict, yet also recognize, create, and take advantage of opportunities for promoting desired change.

Peacebuilding must thus be responsive: It must simultaneously be long-term slow and short-term intensive. We must be able to respond to what is happening now and at the same time connect that response to the vision of desired change. We need, therefore, to view funding and evaluation less in terms of the realization of particular tasks and more in terms of creating the platform from which it is possible to respond creatively to evolving situations. Sustaining the

platform may well matter more than achieving the originally articulated outcome. In peacebuilding we can and should talk about sustaining process-structure, not just about sustaining outcome.

In both of these dilemmas, I prefer to talk about *initiatives* rather
than projects, and *outcomes* rather than results. "Initiative" points to the
idea that something begins, we enter the stream of activity, but it does
not assume a time-bounded approach. "Outcome" suggests that we
look at "what we have come to." In other words, outcomes should be
understood as dynamic—as a process of understanding and learning—
rather than as static results that are seen as products and end points.

The Reporting Dilemma

To be directly involved in peacebuilding activities in settings of violent conflict supposes a certain level of precariousness and risk (as in
danger), and involves balancing very complex relationships. Peacebuilding represents sensitive, delicate, and, at times, very confidential
work where lives are on the line and affected by the actions taken.
When sensitivity, confidentiality, and a capacity to respond appropriately are present over time they help establish and maintain trust.

Reporting, by contrast, is usually thought of in terms of transparency, comprehensiveness, and regularity—in other words, accountability. Perceptions of people involved in the initiatives (both the
staff of the initiating agencies and community participants) affect
and will be affected by what is reported. Thus, accountability can
often find itself in tension with the needs of confidentiality.

Escaping this dilemma, it seems to me, involves finding a way to
link accountability with the demands of confidentiality. Reporting
needs to be conceptualized so that the nature of the work is understood and enhanced but the mechanisms for achieving accountability
are not counterproductive to the very goals pursued. We also need to
discover how to accomplish reporting in a manner that makes community participants feel a sense of ownership. These participants, it
should be remembered, are resources, not recipients.

The Institutional Capacity Dilemma

We often conceive of peacemakers as high-profile individuals. This tendency, coupled with the project-driven nature of funding, frequently

fosters a false image of the deeper nature of peacebuilding. Peace-building in deeply divided societies is, above all, the task of establishing an infrastructure for sustaining initiatives. Although individuals may be highlighted and are certainly a key to peace, institutional capacity building is what makes the difference over time. This is too often overlooked in funding, because it is easier to fund the project than the infrastructure, and because it is easier to measure the result as product than the outcome as process.

OVERVIEW OF EVALUATION APPROACHES

The dilemmas outlined above suggest that as we approach evaluation, we must do so with a framework that is responsive to the unique goals and dynamics of peacebuilding and of the context within which it is carried out. It is not merely a question of assessing easily visible and static outcomes. It is a matter of developing a practical perspective and set of tools that help us see and learn as the process-structure of peacebuilding evolves. Before describing some of these tools, it will be useful to summarize briefly several ideas I have found instructive in their development.

Jay Rothman has proposed a framework for "action evaluation" in the field of conflict resolution based on a methodology of bringing together "formative" and "summative" data.[3] He proposes this approach in order to provide a mechanism for identifying the "baseline" of an initiative elicited from within the value structure of the people involved. Rothman has identified three basic questions aimed at clarifying the goals, motivations, and processes in the initiative. Making these explicit provides a base for tracking and reflecting on the goals and whether they are met—a process that is useful for both internal feedback and external validity. This is accomplished through setting explicit goals with input from stakeholders before the initiative, and from mechanisms tracking progress as the process evolves.

Carol Weiss has provided a parallel approach to what she calls "theory-based" evaluation.[4] Her framework suggests that rather than working with standard evaluation methods, community initiatives should be based on the "theories of change" that underlie the work conducted. Her central idea is that all social programs are based on implicit or explicit theories of change that suggest what will work, what is worth doing, and why. Evaluation, she believes, should bring to the surface these theories and carefully delineate the assumptions on which they rest. Evaluation of these assumptions provides feedback about which theories, or aspects of theories, are best supported by the community's experience. She offers four reasons for doing this. First, it concentrates evaluation resources on key aspects of the initiative. Second, it connects the findings to a broader base of understanding. Third, it asks practitioners to be more explicit about their assumptions, about what they are trying and why. And fourth, evaluations of the theories of change are likely to have wider value for policymakers and practitioners. The primary purpose is not only to do good, but also to *understand* how, when, and why it is being done.

To these two evaluation frameworks we can add an important suggestion from Joyce Hocker and William Wilmot, who have proposed the concepts of prospective, transactive, and retrospective goals in conflict transformation processes.[5] Hocker and Wilmot's central idea is that goals change as conflict, and its associated learning process, evolves. Prospective goals are those that we make explicit before we initiate a process of dealing with a specific conflict. Transactive goals are those that become more apparent as episodes in the conflict develop. Retrospective goals refer to the fact that people continue to try to make sense of what happened long after it has occurred. In many cases, only after the fact are we able to best explain what was going on, how we tried to make sense of it, and what we were trying to do.

Hocker and Wilmot contend that each of these three types of goal should be correlated with content goals and relational goals. Content goals relate to what people want and need in terms of the substance of the conflict. These are often the visible issues we debate, argue, or fight over. Relational goals are those goals that correspond to the questions of who we are to one another: the influence, the distance or proximity, and the level of interdependence that we seek and/or grant one another. Peacebuilding is concerned both with finding ways to deal with the issues in a conflict and with the redefining of relationship.

In all three cases, these authors have identified aspects of evaluation and goal assessment that reinforce aspects of the peacebuilding framework. In terms of evaluation, the key principles articulated by these authors are as follow:

- the need to clarify goals and articulate implicit values;
- the recognition that feedback mechanisms must be interspersed throughout the life of the initiative, and that feedback will further clarify and change goals;
- the need to make explicit the theory of change that undergirds the processes and activities proposed;
- the need for a process of contextualization of the methods and standards for measurement; and
- the need to conduct evaluation in participation with the people engaged in peacebuilding.

WORKING ASSUMPTIONS FOR STRATEGIC AND RESPONSIVE EVALUATION

The dilemmas identified and the suggestions made about evaluation lead to a series of working assumptions that can serve as a point of departure for developing an exploratory set of evaluation tools. These assumptions include the following.

- Peacebuilding is about seeking and sustaining processes of change; it is not exclusively, or even primarily, about sustaining outcomes. Rebuilding societies torn by violence and war involves rebuilding relationships and finding new ways to be in relationship. What we are trying to measure, therefore, is a not a static outcome but a dynamic process.
- Peacebuilding requires changes across multiple levels and perspectives. We must understand, create, and sustain the space for change along a continuum that includes personal, relational, structural, and cultural dimensions.
- Pursuing such a range of change in a society torn by war requires vision and a design for attaining that long-term goal. The design of any process of change is built on some understanding of how

change works and what produces it. A concern for evaluation suggests that we need, therefore, to be more explicit about our often implicit theories of change, which are inherent in the designs and proposals we carry forward.

- Social conflict is based in relationships. It is cyclical and episodic in nature. "Cyclical" refers to the ongoing nature of conflict based in relationships; "episodic" to the patterns of escalation and de-escalation around particular issues. When we approach evaluation we must think about both the longer-term context and the immediate episodes that constitute conflict and its dynamics.

The nature of protracted conflict is represented in figure 10, where conflict is shown as a continuous cycle. Each circle is made up of the ongoing context of relationships and the more time-bound dynamics of specific episodes. I have interjected the Hocker and Wilmot idea that in each episodic cycle prospective, trans-active, and retrospective goals are present. As we come to evaluation, we will need to recognize that the design of peacebuilding is entering an ongoing system of destructive violence.

- Most settings that have experienced deep-rooted, protracted conflict (war, in particular) share certain characteristics and patterns that have developed over many years (indeed, over the course of decades, even generations). These are patterns of social, cultural, political, and systemically sustained violence. Just as these societies have made a long-term investment in organized violence, so the process of effecting change in these settings will require sustained efforts to constructively involve and impact the system and people affected. Indeed, it is likely to take more or less as long to get out of a conflict as it took to get in it. As depicted in figure 10, evaluation will need to take account of an environment characterized by a dynamic ongoing process and context of long-term violent relationships producing cyclical conflict episodes.

- Change in the conflict patterns occurs within a changing environment. There is no such thing as a static social moment. We are seeking change in a dynamic context. This is especially true in postaccord periods, when societies move with great energy and high expectations from war to peace.

- Responsiveness requires a vision of change and practical, immediate action. These two must be held in constant counterbalance. On its own, isolated from the other, neither vision nor action is capable of generating a process for sustainable peace.
- Societal change within a framework of strategic peacebuilding can only be accomplished through sustained initiatives that promote vertical and horizontal integration of people and processes.
- Responsive evaluation needs a continuous cycle of action and reflection.
- When we look for ways to measure peacebuilding outcomes as process-structures, we focus on that which is not immediately visible. Products are visible, but they rarely provide us with strategic indicators. Much more difficult to see are the processes that redefine and rebuild relationship and respond to immediate crises.
- We must be descriptive before we can be prescriptive. We must increase our capacity to describe situations, identifying the key dilemmas around issues and relationships, before we jump to solutions. Dilemma posing is a useful tool to frame a conflict and provide a point of reference for evaluation of specific action.

CREATING STRATEGIC AND RESPONSIVE TOOLS FOR EVALUATION

To move toward strategic and responsive evaluation, we require tools that help us clarify and evaluate the theories of change underlying, and the actions envisaged in, the design for peacebuilding. We must find a way to move from rather abstract ideas to concrete points of inquiry. In the rest of this chapter, I propose a set of tools that will enable us to make this move.

A first tool is simply to map the biggest picture possible. Here we return to figure 10 and the context-episodic nature of protracted conflict. We must attach evaluative work to the realities faced by peacebuilding initiatives in protracted conflicts, recognizing that the initiatives are aimed at change that will take place over years, maybe decades, but that the peacebuilding activities must respond to the immediate context and episodes that emerge from day to day.

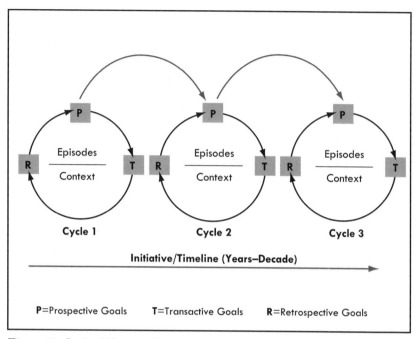

Figure 10. Cyclical Nature of Peacebuilding.

Within the big picture we can now begin to add the specific tools for integrating the strategic and responsive components of evaluation. I suggest that these tools can take the form of six sets of inquiry that are interdependent and circular in their relationship. I describe them here briefly and then suggest a working format in figures 11, 12, 13, 14, and 15.

Inquiry 1: Goals and Assumptions (Figure 11)

As a first step, it will be useful to establish what Rothman referred to as the "baseline," or what we might call the point of entry. From the perspective of the framework for peacebuilding, the baseline requires that we articulate the vision of what is desired and the kind of processes that would embody such a vision. At the beginning of a new initiative, this can be done only from a prospective goal projection. As the initiative moves on and/or as we introduce the evaluative

Timeline: Cycle 1	Situational and Dilemma Assessment	Change Desired	Assumptions
Prospective (Pre-Cycle 1)	Describe the situation and context of conflict in terms of strategic dilemmas: 1. 2. 3. 4.	Describe the change desired in terms of overall goals: 1. 2. 3. 4.	Describe assumptions/values implicit in change desired: 1. 2. 3. 4.
Transactive (Midterm Cycle 1)	How has direct experience changed the assessment? 1. 2. 3. 4.	How has direct experience and assessment revision affected overall goals? 1. 2. 3. 4.	What are the changes in assumptions implicit in goals changes? 1. 2. 3. 4.
Retrospective (End-Cycle 1)	Looking back across the cycle, how has the experience changed the assessment of strategic dilemmas? 1. 2. 3. 4.	Looking back across the cycle, how have goals changed? 1. 2. 3. 4.	Looking back across the cycle, what were the central working assumptions implicit in goals and activities? 1. 2. 3. 4.

Figure 11. Inquiry into Dilemmas, Goals, and Assumptions for Peacebuilding.

inquiry into ongoing processes, we add layers of reflectivity emerging from transactive and retrospective goal perspectives. Moving toward a practical application, our starting point is to develop a baseline that is *descriptive* in nature and includes these three components:

1. Describe the current situation of conflict in terms of key dilemmas.
2. Describe the vision of change that is desired in this setting.
3. Describe the assumptions and values that are implicit in the vision of change.

Inquiry 2: Design and Theories of Change (Figure 12)

This inquiry is concerned with creating the mechanism that helps focus attention on peacebuilding as generating processes that create the space for significant social change. This approach requires a capacity to articulate both the design of social change in radically changing environments and the underlying theories of change of that design. Three components are involved:

1. Describe the processes to be generated in terms of activities that flesh out the goals related to the context and immediate situations faced.
2. Describe the outcomes that are desired at the level of specific content results and relational process.
3. Describe the theory of change that underlies the processes.

Although this is done at a prospective level initially, the dynamic of this set of inquiries is more clearly accomplished through transactive goal evaluation. Here the focus is on how action in the context informs our understanding about the nature of the dilemmas faced, the goals articulated, and the processes needed to respond. Transactive goal evaluation means that we create an ongoing mechanism for action and reflection: We create a space to clarify and re-explain the goals according to what we see happening. It is the space for feedback and change in the initiative that creates the *responsive* contribution of the evaluation. In this case, the three components remain the same, but with the addition of the phrase: "Given what we are learning about this context, the emerging issues, and the changing environment . . ."

Timeline: Cycle 1	Processes	Outcomes	Theories
Prospective	Describe the processes to be generated: 1. 2. 3. 4.	Describe outcomes projected: 1. Personal 2. Relational 3. Structural 4. Cultural	Describe the theories of change implicit in the processes: 1. 2. 3. 4.
Transactive	Given what we now know about this context, the emerging issues, and the changing environment, we now believe these processes are most indicated: 1. 2. 3. 4.	Given what we now know about this context, the emerging issues, and the changing environment, we now believe: 1. Personal 2. Relational 3. Structural 4. Cultural	Given what we now know about this context, the emerging issues, and the changing environment, we now believe: 1. 2. 3. 4.
Retrospective	Looking back across this cycle, these were significant aspects of the process generated in terms of seeking desired change: 1. 2. 3. 4.	Looking back across the cycle, these were the specific outcomes of the initiative: 1. Personal 2. Relational 3. Structural 4. Cultural	Looking back across the cycle, we now see these theories of change: 1. 2. 3. 4.

Figure 12. Inquiry into the Design of Processes and Theories of Change.

Inquiry 3: Strategic Indicators (Figure 13)

This inquiry is concerned with creating a set of indicators that provide feedback on the strategic impact of the activities from the perspective of the peacebuilding framework. Typically in evaluation processes that are driven by a "project" mentality, we look for indicators that are concrete and measurable. For example, if we are interested in improving the availability of drinking water in rural areas, we might measure the results by how many wells have been dug. In the arena of peacebuilding, our dilemma lies with how to create the appropriate categories of indicators. When we think quantitatively, there are aspects of the work that we can verify: the number of training workshops conducted, people who participated, mediations conducted, agreements reached, and so forth. These are helpful for reporting the breadth of activity. However, they tell us very little about the quality of change, or the sustainability of the transformative process. From the perspective of peacebuilding, dynamic social process and change are precisely the elements we seek to understand, promote, and measure, and which represent strategic responsiveness.

Strategic indicators require a set of lenses that help us focus on the progression of desired change at the level of relationship and process. I suggest three categories of indicators that emerge from the peacebuilding framework: vertical/horizontal integration, conjunctural capacity responsiveness, and transformative capacity responsiveness.

Inquiry 4: Vertical/Horizontal Integration

Vertical/horizontal integration is concerned with how the activities have encouraged (and, one hopes, sustained) the development of working relationships that cut across the levels of society vertically (linking community work with higher levels, both within each community and beyond the community) and that cut across the lines of identity that mark the central divisions of the society. These indicators are particularly interested in whether two process-structures exist in the form of

- new processes that have been generated for increasing participation in peacebuilding and creating constructively redefined relationships in the setting; and

Timeline: Cycle 1	Processes	Mechanisms
Prospective	In the activities to be generated, what is the level of participation and development of relationships in the targeted communities/initiatives? 1. Is there significant relationship vertically (between the grass-roots and local/regional/national leadership)? 2. Is there significant relationship horizontally (across the perceived lines of conflict identities)? 3. Who seem to have the greatest potential to serve as agents of change in this setting?	In the activities to be generated: 1. What are the projected mechanisms (institutions/networks) that are to be created? 2. How are they designed to cut across vertical/horizontal levels? 3. What exists that functions well and what support does it need? What exists that does not function well and needs to be changed? What does not exist that should?
Transactive	From direct experience so far: 1. What obstacles are there to achieving vertical/horizontal integration? 2. What steps have been proposed to overcome those obstacles? 3. Who, at this point, appear to have the greatest potential for change (significant people/relationships)?	From direct experience so far: 1. What mechanisms appear to be needed and possible? 2. What would be needed to sustain these mechanisms?
Retrospective	Looking back across the cycle: 1. What obstacles are there in achieving vertical/horizontal integration? 2. What are proposed steps to overcome those obstacles? 3. Who, at this point, appears to have greatest potential for change (significant people/relationships)?	Looking back across the cycle: 1. What mechanisms appear to be needed and possible? 2. What would be needed to sustain these mechanisms? 3. What exists, what needs changing, what needs creating?

Figure 13. Inquiry into Vertical and Horizontal Integration.

- new social mechanisms that are emerging from those processes and that have a life beyond the immediate need that gave them birth.

Inquiry 5: Conjunctural Capacity Responsiveness (Figure 14)

This matrix refers to effectiveness of the activity and the mechanisms created to respond to the immediate crises and issues emerging in the environment of change in a postsettlement context. (In terms of the infrastructure matrix depicted in figure 9, this matrix addresses mainly the content of the *crisis* column.) These issues are often the focal point for much social and political energy. They are experienced as the "real" problems that must be dealt with immediately. The conjunctural capacity will provide indicators that measure the effectiveness of the peacebuilding activity in responding to the perceived needs on crisis issues from the perspective of the people with whom the project is working. A strategically focused conjunctural capacity will raise these retrospective questions:

1. What issues blocked constructive change for this community? (These are considered *strategic* issues.)
2. Was the initiative able to identify these strategic issues at an early stage? Did the initiative miss the strategic issues? What processes of assessment would have helped to identify them earlier?
3. What did the initiative put forward as a response?
4. Did the participating community feel the response was adequate? What do community members say was missed?
5. Did the response help create new processes or mechanisms (see the discussion above of vertical/horizontal integration)?

In each instance, we once again must pay careful attention to the retrospective goals, given that it is often only after full cycles of initiatives have had a chance to run their course that we are able to detect what aspects of the initiative actually held strategic capacity.

Inquiry 6: Transformative Capacity Responsiveness (Figure 15)

This matrix refers to the impact the initiative has displayed in terms of its effect on movement toward articulated longer-term goals in relationship to structural and cultural change—as in moving from a

Timeline: Cycle 1	Strategic Issues	Responses	Feedback
Prospective	What issues could block constructive desired change for this community? 1. 2. 3.	What responses are projected to work with these issues? 1. 2. 3.	Who participated in identifying the issues? How is this linked to vertical/horizontal integration?
Transactive	From direct experience so far, what issues are blocking change? 1. 2. 3.	Describe the processes generated in response to the issues: 1. 2. 3.	Did the participating communities/other levels of society feel the response was adequate? What gaps in response do they identify? Are the processes generated responsive to their concerns?
Retrospective	Looking back across the cycle: 1. What were the strategic issues that needed to be addressed? 2. Did the initiative miss some issues? 3. What process of assessment would have helped to identify them earlier?	Looking back across the cycle, describe the processes generated in response to the issues: 1. 2. 3.	Looking back across the cycle: 1. Did the participating community feel the response was adequate? 2. What gaps in response did they identify? 3. Were strategic mechanisms generated?

Figure 14. Inquiry into Conjunctural Capacity Responsiveness.

culture of violence and separation to a culture of interdependence and dialogue. (In terms of the infrastructure matrix depicted in figure 9, this matrix links the third and fourth columns, which are concerned with creating space for a shared vision of the future and the institutional changes and capacities necessary to move toward that vision.) In particular, the focus is on gaining access to the subsystem level. Transformative capacity raises these kind of questions, from a retrospective goal perspective:

1. Was space created for community members to engage in a process of imaging their common future?
2. Which central institutions and networks were involved or changed (or were not involved or blocked desired change) at the community level? Was the initiative able to identify these strategic subsystems? What processes of assessment would help to identify them at an earlier stage?
3. What was (or would appear to be) the level of intervention in the system (local, subsystem, national) that holds the greatest potential for desired change? Was this identified? Are there processes for early detection?
4. Does the community feel necessary structural changes are taking place? What do they feel is missing? How does this relate to the common vision of the future and the subsystem goals?

CONCLUSION

This chapter has suggested that evaluation in the field of peacebuilding can be approached within a strategic and responsive framework. For that to happen, however, tools and indicators must be developed that help highlight the strategic nature of activities undertaken in the process of creating an infrastructure to support peacebuilding. That infrastructure should emerge from the realities in the setting and be oriented toward making visible the desired processes of changes.

Seen from this perspective, evaluation is understood as a circular mix of design, feedback, and systematization of learning that emerges from and returns to the work, rather than as a tool oriented toward

Timeline: Cycle 1	Vision	Potential for Change	Feedback
Prospective	Describe how the initiative will create space for articulating a common vision for peace emerging from the setting.	Identify the institutions/networks that need to be involved in that vision and the change it will require. At the subsystem level, what networks/institutions hold the greatest capacity for desired change? Describe how they will be engaged in the process.	Describe how the community will be engaged in providing feedback about these changes.
Transactive	With direct experience, how is the vision for desired change proposed in terms of subsystem and structural levels? 1. 2. 3.	With direct experience, describe: 1. What networks/institutions hold the greatest capacity for desired change? 2. How they will be engaged in the process?	How is feedback obtained from participants in the community? Do participants feel that structural/subsystem changes are taking place? What are the gaps in their opinion?
Retrospective	Looking back across the cycle, how was the vision understood and/or modified after the experience?	Looking back across the cycle, describe: 1. What networks/institutions held the greatest capacity for desired change? 2. What blocked their participation?	Looking back across the cycle: 1. Did participants feel that structural/subsystem changes took place? 2. What were the gaps in their opinion? 3. What were the points of progress?

Figure 15. Inquiry into Transformative Capacity Responsiveness.

measuring final results. A process-oriented evaluative approach underlines the necessity of developing the capacities to identify and articulate key dilemmas facing people in the setting, to design strategic initiatives that integrate vertical and horizontal potentials in the society, and to respond to immediate emerging issues in a manner that lays the groundwork for transforming the subsystem and achieving structural change in the broader society.

11

CONCLUSION

● ● ●

In the preceding chapters I have outlined a perspective on peace-building in divided societies. It starts from the premise that contemporary conflict presents us, as an international community, with a number of critical challenges. Peacebuilding, it was argued, must face and adapt to the realities and dilemmas posed by the very nature of these conflicts.

The global overview and delineation of the characteristics of contemporary conflict established the dilemmas and challenges confronting peacebuilding in deeply divided societies. We are faced with systemic issues of how to deal with the production, transfer, and ready availability of weapons for warmaking, which fuel and make possible an extraordinary level of armed violence. This effect is compounded by a general international tolerance of the resort to armed struggle and defense as a means for dealing with political, economic, and socio-cultural differences.

The outward expression of this systemic pattern is the active unfolding of more than forty armed conflicts that can be classified as wars. For the most part, these are internal rather than international conflicts, built around identity groups and often characterized as ethnic and/or religious in nature. These conflicts often erupt as expressions of accumulated pain, with marked emotional and psychological patterns of nearly institutionalized hatred and division. The immediacy of the suffering and fear that accompany war reinforces the historic enmity.

These are truly deep-rooted conflicts, which pose for us two central questions: What conceptual framework is most useful for dealing with the structural and psychosocial nature of contemporary conflict? What practical approaches and activities have the greatest potential for moving these conflicts toward, and for sustaining, peaceful outcomes?

I have argued that an answer might well lie in the development of a comprehensive, integrative, strategic approach to the transformation of conflict. This approach is built on a conceptual framework composed of an interdependent set of perspectives and activities identified as structure, process, reconciliation, resources, and coordination.

The discussion of structure was concerned with the systemic elements of how one approaches a setting of protracted conflict. Two sets of lenses were provided to help focus attention on (1) the levels of peacebuilding activity across the affected population, and (2) how the sources of conflict in a given setting are connected to conflict dynamics in the system within which the conflict is located. Structure also relates to pressing macro issues, such as disarmament, that go beyond the scope of a particular context.

The discussion of process brought into focus the long-term nature of the progression of conflict. It suggested the need to develop an adequate time frame in the conceptualization of the practice of peacebuilding, and to envision and provide space for multiple roles and functions in the transformation of conflict toward sustainable peace.

The discussion of reconciliation stressed that relationship, in its full range of psychosocial dimensions, is central to transformation. Reconciliation is promoted by providing space and opportunity for encounters at various levels, bringing together people from opposing sides and encouraging them to articulate their past pain and to envision an interdependent future.

The discussion of resources noted that although financial support is of course necessary, yet more important is the development of new ways of thinking about categories, responsibilities, and strategic commitment to peacebuilding, and of a new understanding of the sociocultural resources present in a conflict setting. A critical element in resourcing is to target funding at times and in ways that contribute to long-term transformation at the level both of prevention and of postconflict social reconstruction. No less important a task is to develop a framework within which a peace constituency can be identified and built.

The discussion of coordination emphasized the need to have specific mechanisms whereby the above four components can intersect, interact, and cross-fertilize. Coordination is seen more as a function of communication and creating points of contact than as a matter of centralizing management of the peace process.

Several basic proposals lie at the heart of the framework and argument presented here.

First, I have suggested that the nature of contemporary conflict requires the development of theories and praxis of the "middle range." I have outlined some examples of such approaches. Specifically, I have proposed that middle-range actors within the population are uniquely situated to have the greatest potential for constructing an infrastructure for peace. They have the capacity to impact processes and people at both the top and the grassroots levels. If mobilized strategically for peacebuilding, middle-range leaders could lay the foundation for long-term, sustainable conflict transformation. It is at this level, therefore, that innovative and intensive strategies—a "middle-out" approach—must be encouraged and supported.

Second, I have proposed the need for "subsystem" strategies that link immediate issues within the setting to the broader systemic dynamics within which the particular conflict unfolds. We must not ignore the systemic issues—such as arms production and transfer, disarmament, demobilization, and the reconstruction of civil societies—but we cannot tackle these macro issues from the sanctuary of intellectual discussion and broad, but often powerless, international policy statements. We must develop specific initiatives and projects that deal with these issues in relation to the immediate situations affected by them. This, again, suggests a long-term view of process, but one that is coupled with movement toward immediate action.

Third, I have maintained that reconciliation is a central component of dealing with contemporary conflict and reconstructing divided societies. Reconciliation is understood as a process of relationship building. Thus, reconciliation is not limited to the period of postsettlement restoration. Rather, reconciliation is seen as providing a focus and a locus appropriate to every stage of peacebuilding and instrumental in reframing the conflict and the energies driving the conflict.

Fourth, I have argued that innovation is needed in approaching the core nature of deep-rooted conflict in divided societies. To rebuild relationships, we must develop innovative ways of providing space within which the emotional and psychological aspects of the conflict can be addressed. Traditional approaches to diplomacy have tended to see reconciliation as peripheral, or worse, as irrelevant to the substance of building peace, when in fact reconciliation is the ingredient with the capacity to create the conditions for proactive, sustainable change.

Finally, I have argued that coordination must be a central component in the effective implementation of a comprehensive peacebuilding strategy and in the building of an infrastructure for peace. Coordination facilitates the cross-fertilization of the various elements, levels of work, and activities across the progression of conflict in a given setting. Armed conflicts in deeply divided societies represent complex, long-term challenges; if these challenges are to be met, a multiplicity of roles and functions, approaches and activities must be brought into play. Peacebuilding efforts and initiatives must have points of contact and be coordinated if the constructive transformation of a conflict is to be sustained. This calls for not only an understanding of the larger challenge but also an acknowledgment of the need for a multiplicity of roles, for multiple levels of activity, and for diverse strategies and approaches, each with a distinctive contribution to make.

In conclusion, building peace requires a comprehensive approach to contemporary conflict. We need a conceptual framework that helps us envision the overall picture and moves us toward specific action and activity. Our challenge is to find strategic and practical approaches that help establish an infrastructure for sustainable transformation and that take seriously the immediate and deep-rooted needs of divided societies. We are not impaired by a lack of resources, if we choose to invest wisely and practically in peace. We are limited only by how far we are willing to cast our vision. We must not despair at the depth and breadth of the challenge, but rather rise to meet it. Reconciliation is possible. The house of peace can be built.

APPLYING CONCEPTS TO CASES: FOUR AFRICAN CASE STUDIES

by John Prendergast

● ● ●

John Paul Lederach has formulated a series of excellent conceptual frameworks for analyzing sources of conflict, actors in conflict and conflict resolution, approaches to multilevel peacebuilding, and transformative approaches to training. This chapter will attempt to enrich these four frameworks with case material from four African countries—Sudan, Ethiopia, Rwanda, and Somalia—whose histories are pockmarked by chronic conflict and instability, and which have tried an assortment of methods to manage their social, political, and economic divisions.

ACTORS AND APPROACHES TO PEACEBUILDING: THE CASE OF SUDAN

Lederach employs the model of a pyramid (see figure 2, page 39) to depict the leading actors in a population affected by a conflict. At the apex of the pyramid are the highly visible top-level leaders or actors—key political and military leaders, for the most part. Below them are the middle-level leaders, who are drawn from such fields as religion, academia, and the arts, and who are connected to both the top level and the grassroots but who are neither bound by the political calculations that govern the actions of the former nor encumbered by the survival demands facing the latter. At the bottom of the pyramid is the grassroots leadership, a group with firsthand knowledge of the struggle for survival and the local expression of deep-rooted animosity between identity groups. Grassroots actors include members of indigenous NGOs working with local populations, refugee camp leaders, health officials, and so on.

Sudan provides a window into a better understanding of Lederach's pyramidal model. The country has been at war for three of the past four decades. A peace agreement brokered largely by the World Council of Churches ended one round of fighting in 1972, but the war resumed with a vengeance in 1983. Since then, a host of initiatives aimed at settling the conflict have been launched that have involved either top-level (level-one), middle-level (level-two), or grassroots (level-three) leaders. This analysis will focus on efforts made since 1989, when the current Sudanese regime came to power in a military coup initiated by the National Islamic Front (NIF), a radical political Islamist group closely connected to extremist organizations from the Middle East and with an agenda that prioritizes expansion southward into sub-Saharan Africa.[1] The preponderant focus on levels one and three in the following analysis reflects the conscious disempowerment of level-two actors by Sudanese government and rebel authorities, as well as a lack of focus by the international community on those actors.

Level One

Top-level actors from the Sudanese government side have primarily been officials with strong connections and loyalty to the NIF. On the opposition side, until 1991 the sole representatives at peace talks have been officials of the Sudan People's Liberation Movement/Army (SPLM/A), the main rebel group in southern Sudan. When in 1991 a faction splintered from the SPLM/A—that faction is now called the South Sudan Independence Movement/Army (SSIM/A) —it became incorporated into diplomatic efforts to end the larger war, to reduce interfactional fighting among southern rebel groups, and to expand humanitarian access for aid agencies. Northern opposition groups—both armed and unarmed, both sectarian and secular— are also key top-level actors, but they have not been involved in internationally mediated peace efforts.

Level-one approaches to building peace have revolved around negotiations between the government and rebel groups brokered by parties in and outside Africa. A number of external players, including the Organization of African Unity (OAU) and the U.S. State Department, have attempted to broker cease-fires or peace agreements with the warring parties. Most of these efforts have produced little forward movement or innovation, although they have expanded contacts and dialogue among the conflicting groups. Three initiatives deserve further elaboration.

The first significant initiative is that of the Inter-Governmental Authority on Development (IGAD), the regional organization that addresses issues of common concern to Horn of Africa countries. The IGAD Initiative on Sudan held a series of negotiating sessions in 1993 and 1994 with the Sudanese government, the SPLM/A, and the SSIM/A. The initiative culminated in the crafting of a Declaration of Principles (DOP), which laid out the terms upon which the Sudanese civil war could be resolved, and addressed the central issues of religion's role in the state and the opportunity for self-determination for marginalized Sudanese peoples, particularly southerners. The government appeared to accept the DOP, but in a mid-1994 session abruptly turned tail and reneged on the agreement, condemning the process as biased toward the southern rebels. Since then, the DOP has remained the standard from which other initiatives must begin, and the IGAD countries (particularly Ethiopia, Eritrea, and Uganda) have adopted a parallel military strategy of containment against Sudanese incursions into their countries.[2]

These three regional governments are firmly convinced that the NIF remains committed to regional Islamization, and—unlike some representatives of the diplomatic community—they do not believe that moderates within the Sudanese regime can alter or reform the NIF's agenda. These governments are committed to a three-track policy: support for negotiations within the framework of the IGAD Initiative; leadership in international efforts to increase multilateral pressure on Khartoum through UN sanctions; and coordination among themselves and with the Sudanese opposition in their attempts to militarily defeat the NIF regime. A unique combination of diplomatic pressure, military intervention, and support for further negotiation results.

The promise of the IGAD Initiative is greater when seen in the context of IGAD's larger agenda of enhancing food security and conflict prevention in the Horn. As the organization matures, further integration between its various mandates will inevitably occur, providing opportunities for consequent integration of level-one, level-two, and level-three initiatives.

Two other interesting top-level interventions involve a neighboring government and a former U.S. president. In the first case, Eritrea has hosted a series of meetings of the major opposition forces from Sudan in a successful effort to unify their platforms and coordinate their strategies. (The process is partly driven by the logic that a united opposition will be better prepared to bring eventual peace to Sudan and the region.) In the second case, former President Jimmy Carter has involved himself in efforts to negotiate cease-fires for humanitarian reasons. His most successful intervention took place in 1995, when he was able to negotiate a temporary cessation of hostilities in the south among the three major parties to the war in order to expand efforts to contain the deadly guinea worm disease. The cease-fire was often violated, but never seriously, and humanitarian aid agencies found it easier to secure access than before the cessation of fighting.

Level Two

Middle-level actors in Sudan include authority figures from a number of social groups: Islamic leaders in various communities in northern Sudan; Christian leaders from various denominations in southern Sudan; union leaders, who have mostly been driven underground but still retain a significant following within northern Sudan; and prominent exiles who have varying degrees of association with the warring parties. Initiatives involving these actors are somewhat limited, however, chiefly because of the systematic elimination of middle-level leadership by the warring parties and the top-down control they maintain in the areas of their control (the SSIM/A is an exception in this regard, due to its style of authority and tenuous control of the areas in which it operates).

Nonetheless, a variety of efforts have been made to open or maintain communication among level-two figures. For instance:

• Southern Sudanese church leaders within the New Sudan Council of Churches consortium have sought to maintain contacts between middle-level actors from the conflicting parties; similar efforts have been made by a group of exiled southern politicians under the banner of the United Sudan African Parties.

- An IGAD Resource Group has brought together a handful of Sudan experts to assist the larger IGAD Initiative on Sudan.
- The All Africa Conference of Churches sponsors a Sudan Working Group, which brings together a global network of churches in support of a mechanism in Nairobi that encourages peacemaking in Sudan. Formed in 1993, the working group is headed unofficially by an eminent retired Kenyan diplomat, Bethuel Kiplagat. The Sudan Working Group maintains contacts with the warring parties in Sudan, donor governments, IGAD, and a variety of NGOs interested in conflict resolution in Sudan.
- UNICEF (the United Nations Children's Fund), the United Nations Development Programme (UNDP), and the UN Department of Humanitarian Affairs consistently engage in humanitarian diplomacy that involves actors other than the top-level warlords, in the hopes of improving the delivery of humanitarian aid and the prospects for peace. Efforts in these directions take the form of quiet diplomacy, capacity building of midlevel officials of the "humanitarian wings" of the warring parties, and problem-solving fora such as UNDP's conference in 1996 that promoted peace-building through enhanced cooperation on relief and development.

Problem-solving workshops, conflict resolution training, and other such initiatives involving segments of society not representing warring parties are limited. Because of strong external backing for the southern Sudanese churches, efforts are occasionally made to bring church leaders together to talk about peace. By and large, however, such initiatives are frustrated by the fact that sectoral leaders have been sidelined or driven underground or into exile by the warring parties.

Level Three

Grassroots leaders in Sudan are first and foremost the traditional authorities in their areas: the chiefs, cattle camp leaders, traditional religious prophets, sheikhs, and elders. The traditional authorities within the south hold great potential for future peace efforts, based on their historical role in managing conflict between warring pastoral communities. The chiefs retain key functions, such as maintaining traditions, providing witness, and negotiating blood money payments *(diya)*.

A process of disempowerment of traditional authorities in southern Sudan has resulted in part from policies by the Sudan government and the SPLM/A, both of which have sought to circumvent traditional power structures. Even so, since the Chukudum Convention of 1994, the SPLM/A has slowly begun to restore the authority of the chiefs at the local level in many districts, particularly through the reestablishment of chiefs' courts to dispense customary law.

Those Sudanese involved in relief and development work—whether with international or with local organizations—have acquired authority by virtue of the resources they appear to control and the salaries they receive. Despite having a lower social standing than the traditional authorities, these actors nevertheless are an increasingly important local-level leadership category.

As the following examples illustrate, the greatest vitality and innovation in peacebuilding are to be found at the grassroots level, with diverse responses and initiatives being undertaken that involve both external agencies and internal actors.

• In Sudan, an estimated twenty thousand children have been separated from their parents or guardians over the course of the civil war. Without the security of home or family, these children have been forced to fend for themselves, and have shifted frequently from one temporary camp to another as fighting has raged in Sudan and in neighboring Ethiopia, where many sought refuge. Most of these unaccompanied children have trekked hundreds of miles before settling in isolated communities.[3]

The unaccompanied minors are virtually all boys between eight and sixteen years old. In 1988, after the war in the south escalated, thousands walked toward Ethiopia from western Upper Nile and Bahr el Ghazal, hundreds of kilometers away. Most lived in the Sudanese refugee camps at Itang, Panyido, and Dima in western Ethiopia, until they were forced to flee back to Sudan when the Mengistu regime in Ethiopia fell in mid-1991.

With their focus on "vulnerable groups," aid agencies inevitably have been drawn to war-affected children. Globally, the provision of psychosocial services has become a critical component of a holistic response to complex emergencies. Magne Raundelen, a leading child psychologist, helped develop the psychosocial program in southern Sudan. A UNICEF/NGO program is training teachers to recognize symptoms of post-traumatic stress disorder (PTSD) and intervene appropriately.

Although not a high priority for many donors, family reunification has been the object of significant efforts by UNICEF and a number of NGOs. Much research has shown that a child's emotional stability is best guaranteed by being with his or her family. When families are separated, emotional well-being is destroyed and infant mortality can rise quickly.[4] Family-related factors that might impact the psychosocial response of a child include the level of intactness of a family (considered the best defense for children), the degree of nurturing support from the family, and the ability of the family to sustain itself.[5]

- A variety of experiments have been tried with local peace monitoring and peace commissions. In April 1994, for instance, the New Sudan Council of Churches trained local peace monitors in Kenya in interpositioning to strengthen cease-fires and peace agreements, and ultimately to develop institutional capabilities to peacefully transform local conflicts. Following the Ikotos Conference (a peace initiative that addressed intercommunal violence in the Equatoria region of southern Sudan), Bishop Paride Taban of the Catholic Diocese of Torit in southern Sudan formed an association of peace scouts to act as a peace monitoring mechanism in support of the Ikotos agreement. Sixty monitors were selected from numerous villages. The scouts are charged with reporting violations of the Ikotos agreement to the elders of the village. Similarly, in May 1995, the southern Sudanese Episcopal Diocese of Maridi, led by Rev. Joseph Marona, held a local peace conference during which the community chose sixty people to act as peace monitors.

Another local peace committee effort followed the Akobo Peace Conference (an initiative of community elders in southern

Sudan to address intercommunal conflict between two sections of the Nuer people). Mobile peace committees were formed that included community and church leaders, who were tasked with traveling to fishing holes and cattle camps to explain, monitor, and promote the peace agreement. The agreement was commemorated in various locations by reenacting the covenant's sealing and sacrificing animals. Since the conference, small peace meetings have been held throughout the Upper Nile region, during which traditional methods of conflict resolution have been discussed. Local Sudanese women's organizations have been instrumental in moving this process forward in many places. Women's leadership potential has been consciously developed, building the confidence and elevating the status of women's organizations.[6]

- The Akobo Peace Conference was also a key example of one of the most important tools available to grassroots leaders in Sudan: the local peace conference. A study of the Akobo Peace Conference funded by the United States Institute of Peace generated a variety of lessons for indigenous peace processes, among them the importance of employing traditional conflict mechanisms and of involving a wide range of leaders (traditional, military, administrative, and religious), women's groups and leaders, and others with moral authority in the community. The study stressed that external support should be minimal and not replace the indigenous leadership. Indigenous processes represent long-term interactions between traditional and modern societies, and cannot act as quick fixes; they must be placed firmly in historical context for the participants and outside observers.[7]

- Local dispute resolution mechanisms are yet another indigenous, grassroots-level effort to manage conflict and build peace. Traditional courts at the local level are usually stabilizing influences within and between communities. In some parts of southern and central Sudan, communities are reviving their culture by solidifying and updating traditional law—their reason for doing so is to combat the breakdown of order and values that has accompanied the endless civil war and that has been intensified by the intercommunal and interfactional fighting that has plagued the region since 1991.

In Nuer areas of Upper Nile, especially since the Akobo Peace Conference, the chiefs have been reasserting their authority in the area of customary law, with the support of some SSIM/A commanders. In these areas, the concept of *cieng naath*—or covenanting—is a key mechanism for solving conflict in the family, as well as between larger social groups (indeed, it was used in the Akobo Conference).[8] In Lotuko areas in Eastern Equatoria, community leaders are updating, monitoring, and enforcing customary law in the context of the locally initiated process of *emwara* (reconciliation). In Xande areas in Western Equatoria, a museum of culture has been established and interest in traditional law has increased. In some of these areas, soldiers can now be taken to court when they commit civil offenses.

In Dinka areas of southern Bahr al-Ghazal, there is a reassertion of the authority of chiefs' courts as the SPLM/A slowly liberalizes. (One Dinka executive chief in the area points out, "We are the opposite of the Nuer. We want to have broader discussion than just the chiefs. I don't want any one person making the law.")[9] In the context of a fledgling grassroots peace process between Nuer and Dinka communities throughout early 1995, border chiefs on both sides reasserted their authority.

THE NESTED PARADIGM OF CONFLICT FOCI:
THE CASE OF ETHIOPIA

Lederach draws on the work of peace researcher Maire Dugan to help focus on the structural components of an analytical framework for conflict transformation. Dugan has developed a model of a "nested paradigm" (see figure 3, page 56) made up of four levels or elements: issue, relationship, subsystem, and system. This model, Lederach comments, illustrates the need to analyze not only (1) the immediate issues in a conflict, but also (2) the relationships involved, (3) the subsystem in which the problem is directly situated, and (4) the broader systemic concerns, and the responses to each of these levels.

An excellent case study of this nested paradigm is Ethiopia. From the early 1960s, multiple wars of liberation engulfed the country. In

1991, the Eritrean People's Liberation Front (EPLF) pushed Ethiopian troops out of Eritrea and initiated a process that led to independence two years later. The remainder of Ethiopia came under the rule of the Ethiopian People's Revolutionary Democratic Front (EPRDF), an umbrella coalition dominated by Tigrayans from northern Ethiopia whose leadership of the country has been formalized by elections that were boycotted by major opposition parties. Post–civil war Ethiopia is still plagued by localized conflict in certain regions, as well as by national-level tensions brought about by the change in government.

Issue

Immediate tensions are exacerbated by the withdrawal of the major parties from the electoral process in Ethiopia, and the support being provided to certain disaffected groups in Ethiopia by politically oriented radical Islamist elements in Sudan and the Middle East.

In response to the disengagement of the parties, Western donor countries have launched numerous diplomatic initiatives. A group of ambassadors in Addis Ababa was instrumental in brokering a short-lived agreement between the EPRDF ruling party and the Oromo Liberation Front (OLF), the largest opposition group in the country. The agreement broke down over issues of encampment and demobilization of forces. Throughout the transition process from 1991 to 1995, carrots were offered to the opposition parties to return to the elections, but to no avail. When the transition period ended in 1995, the parties that had withdrawn from elections still remained outside the electoral process; the government has moved forward with its agenda of decentralization and development without their participation.

The response to the radical Islamist groups is intertwined with efforts—described in the preceding section—to contain the NIF regime in Sudan. Ethiopia, Eritrea, and Uganda are actively coordinating a multitrack approach to eliminating what they perceive to be the source of their externally inspired problems: the Sudanese government. Negotiations, economic pressure, and military containment are all part of the strategy.

Relationship

Relations between ethnic groups (called "nationalities" in Ethiopia) are predictably complex in a land that sports over eighty different languages. A history of highlander-lowlander competition corresponds with ethnic, religious, and economic divisions. Another enduring rivalry is played out among some of the main highlander groups, with the Tigrayans being currently ascendant. The historically dominant Amhara elite feel completely excluded from the current power structure, as do segments of the historically marginalized Oromo, Somali, and southern Ethiopian political elite.

Peacebuilding responses at the relationship level have been varied. In dealing with interethnic rivalries, local peace conferences have been employed, particularly in the Somali region on the eastern border with Somalia. The Qabri Dahar conference brought together a significant cross-section of the political and traditional leadership of the Ogaden. The conference helped stop the planting of land mines, reduced tensions between the army and local population, drew many of the Ogadeni National Liberation Front (ONLF) rebel fighters out of the bush, increased commerce, and temporarily created some consensus about the future of the region.

Gender relations and the role of women in Ethiopian political life are relational issues of which a peacebuilding strategy should be aware. In April 1995, the Addis Ababa–based NGO InterAfrica Group (IAG) held a workshop on "Women and the Making of Regional Constitutions." IAG brought together fifty women from five regions within Ethiopia to discuss the role of regional women's bureaus, NGO policies related to women at the regional level, and women's involvement in the making of the national and regional constitutions. This kind of focused intervention is more valuable than more systemic recommendations, which sound promising but overwhelm local traditions and thus prove unworkable. In other words, grandiose schemes of gender equity often remain stalled at the rhetorical stage, whereas specific initiatives that build on local or national priorities—as in the case of the involvement of women in the Ethiopian political system—hold much greater chance of success and can provide the building blocks for a more realistic effort at social transformation.

Traditional social organizations that restore and buttress broken relationships are often the means by which local communities resolve conflicts. In Ethiopia, the largest and most influential indigenous formal associations are Eddir, Equb, and Mehaber. Eddir is a welfare institution; Equb is a savings association; and Mehaber is a mechanism for communal responsibility.[10] All of these associations provide avenues for intergroup or intragroup reconciliation. In Sidama areas of southern Ethiopia, Sidama women followed a traditional practice when they tied their undergarments together and laid them between conflicting parties to urge a cessation of hostilities.

Conflict management training in Ethiopia often focuses on healing relationships as a step toward larger peacebuilding goals. ABuGiDa, an indigenous Ethiopian NGO, has organized training sessions in conflict management for community leaders and party members. The Ad Hoc Committee for Peace and Development has held workshops in Harar, South Arssi, Wollaita, and Wollega at which elders and party officials met and discussed their differences.

Subsystem and System

These two levels are interconnected by the structural impediments to peace in Ethiopia. With a population as diverse and a resource base as limited as Ethiopia's, conflict is inevitable. Chronic poverty and over-centralized government underlie all other causes of conflict.

Endemic poverty and wide inequalities of income are often reliable predictors of conflict throughout the Horn. Poverty severely limits opportunities in education, access to resources and livelihoods, and economic advancement.

Food insecurity is inextricably linked with poverty as a root cause of violence.[11] "Food security dominates everything," notes an Ethiopian observer. "People are on a knife-edge of survival."[12] Ironically, policymakers often consider food security to be less political an issue than issues of governance and conflict resolution. But when combined with deep social and economic inequalities, the struggle for scarce resources—especially food—can be a major contributor to violent conflict. Young men from food-insecure regions who face limited livelihood opportunities are the pawns in the power struggles defining most conflicts in the Horn. When these factors are further combined with increased urbanization and thus increased urban poverty, early warning signals for potential conflict and violence should be sounded.

Conflict is also fueled by governance issues. The historical legacies of overcentralized empire and military dictatorship—built by conquest and sustained through divide-and-rule tactics—make governance in contemporary Ethiopia a high-wire act. One of the primary underlying causes of conflict in Ethiopia and the surrounding region is competition over, access to, and distribution of the regional resource pool. The central role of the state in determining resource distribution makes it a major target of, and—when power is overcentralized—a major reason for, conflict.[13]

Given this conflict causality chain marked principally by poverty and overcentralization, the two most effective elements of a peace-building strategy for Ethiopia at the subsystem and system levels are poverty reduction and decentralization.[14]

To counter Ethiopia's chronic food insecurity and low agricultural productivity (as well as to cement its strategic alliance with the peasantry), the Ethiopian government has committed itself to improving smallholder food security, a pledge which if fulfilled should positively impact poverty rates. The foundation of the strategy to increase food production comes from the Green Revolution approach of Global 2000, which features the provision of seeds, technology, rural credit, and fertilizers.

There are a number of rationales for rapidly increasing fertilizer use: fertilizer use has been adopted and has boosted production throughout northeast Africa, but Ethiopia has been slow to follow suit; small farmers have a great interest in using more fertilizers, particularly in the face of increased producer prices and land pressures; fertilizer use is shown to increase yields; and the ability to move fertilizers to farmers is improving.[15] A recent UN study concludes that "fertilizer use is of paramount importance to the future welfare of Ethiopia."[16]

Yields have increased in some areas, but preliminary anecdotal evidence of the effects of the Global 2000 strategy on resource-poor farmers in Ethiopia points up negative impacts in terms of sustainability, as well as increased indebtedness and marginalization of poorer farmers. Inefficient, monopolized, or nonfunctioning market mechanisms distort the effects of increased production, as deficit areas are often not able to afford to buy from surplus areas, even as the price plummets from increased supply. The depressed prices contribute to discouraging farmers from using fertilizer on certain crops. (Longer-term issues found in other countries adopting Green Revolution tactics include environmental degradation, further marginalization of female subsistence farmers, and land consolidation by higher-producing farmers.)

Although fertilizer use and crop production have risen nationally, it is still the case that over 40 percent of Ethiopian peasants have never used fertilizer, only 1 percent of Ethiopia's land is irrigated, 65 percent of smallholders do not sell grain, nearly 40 percent farm less than one-half of a hectare, and half of these small producers are forced to purchase food for their own consumption. Poverty is the primary reason why fertilizer is not more widely used.[17] Risk aversion comes with the territory; children may die if the wrong decisions are made.[18]

Dramatic increases in national-level production are equated with improved food security, ignoring localized food insecurity caused by weaknesses in entitlement and access. The Global 2000 strategy is appropriate for surplus-producing areas, but the government is applying this surplus strategy to the entire country, even though only 35 percent of peasants actually sell surplus grain. The vast majority are extremely vulnerable to fluctuations in prices and climate, and although they could greatly benefit from the production stimulants, their well-founded fear of the weather leads them to be very conservative in their production choices. Thus, they require some assurance that they will not become further indebted (and impoverished) if yields are poor.

The emphasis on productivity diverts Ministry of Agriculture resources away from protecting small farmers who do not have access to inputs, including pesticides and improved seeds. An Ethiopian NGO leader notes, "The program only really helps the middle-level peasants, those with oxen and plentiful labor. But a high percentage of the peasants in Ethiopia do not own oxen. There is no trickle down."[19] Ultimately, if these early problems are not addressed, marginalization and poverty will deepen, creating fertile ground for promoters of violence and revolution.

In addressing the historic overcentralization of the Ethiopian nation-state, the Ethiopian government's main policy—designed to prevent conflict—has been the development of its decentralization agenda. Although the EPRDF introduced a multiparty system in 1991, it was never the party's highest priority. The national election process was largely window-dressing, while the EPRDF proceeded with its own vision of democratization. The electoral processes have been in many ways a distraction from the real processes of decentralization and "ethnic federalism," which devolve power and administrative responsibilities to ethnically demarcated regions, and which are aimed at restructuring the Ethiopian state and replacing the former elites.

The Ethiopian state had been overcentralized for decades. To move forward with any process of political liberalization, the EPRDF had to dismantle that centralized empire-state. If the EPRDF had let go of the reins of power in certain regions, the country may have splintered. In the absence of reliable alliances with the older regional and nationalist parties, the EPRDF needed to rely on satellite allies to maintain control over the process of decentralization. Given that the ethnic federal system is a central component of the government's political program, its effects are being widely debated inside and outside Ethiopia.

One line of analysis critiques the government for not allowing electoral democracy a full chance. Proponents of this line of argument maintain that Ethiopia is a single-party–dominated state in which the imbalances of power at the national and regional levels make it difficult or impossible for other major parties to reenter the democratic process.

Critics also contend that ethnic federalism threatens peace, fails to protect minority rights in the regions, reduces cross-regional movement of people and goods, limits cross-regional labor migration because of restrictions on non-native ethnic hiring, undergirds desires for separation by some groups, and widens divisions among different groups living in the same region. Some analysts charge that what formerly was culturally expressed ethnicity—religion, rituals, festivals, language, and so forth—has become politicized to the degree that it now serves as an ideology of opposition and exclusion. (The OLF and ONLF certainly exploit the divisive elements of this ideology.) Even some of the less visibly contentious elements of ethnic federalism have been criticized by opponents of the policy. For example, Ethiopian government education policies allow the use of local languages in schools. But there is concern that students who learn in their local language will be handicapped by their lack of training in Amhara, English, or other languages of more utility nationally or internationally.[20]

The implementation of the decentralization process provided further fuel for EPRDF critics. Contradictory statements and inadequate information marked the early stages of the process, creating confusion about what powers would actually be granted to local-level administrative units. Few connections were established between the federal reforms and other major reform processes being introduced by the transitional government,[21] and too little forethought was given to dealing with the problems associated with policy, regulation, personnel, communications, provision of services, generation and division of revenue, and budget allocation.[22] A critique by the Economist Intelligence Unit charges that political loyalty to the ruling party is more important than ethnic identity.[23]

Another, more optimistic framework of analysis lauds the participatory structures the government is developing at the local level, as well as the process of devolving administrative power away from the center. A 1995 World Bank study found that much progress had been achieved in enhancing human resource capacity and supporting local administrative structures.[24]

Supporters of ethnic federalism, who regard overcentralization as impractical in such a large and populous country, are encouraged by the government's recognition of local languages and cultures. According to these defenders of the government's policy, the government views ethnic federalism as a means, not an end; it represents an attempt to avert domination by a single ethnic group and to prevent a single economic class from dominating the poor majority. The hope is that if the economy is decentralized, the political arena will change to reflect that new reality, and local development and enterprise will be assisted. Supporters also laud the vision of political participation shared by governments such as those in Ethiopia, Uganda, and Eritrea—a vision quite different from the models advocated by proponents of strict multipartyism.

Resource constraints are enormous. Future problems therefore will likely center around land disputes, the contest between regional governments and the central government over taxing power (the federal government collects 85 percent of domestically generated revenue, 90 percent if foreign aid is included),[25] and the transfer of funds from the center to the regions.

The regionalization policy has localized conflict that might have been directed at the national level. During the violent early transition of 1991–93, ethnic cleansing was carried out at the local level, and power struggles were played out locally. Many residents considered not native to a particular area were burned out of their homes. More recent tactics of ethnic cleansing are less violent, involving, for example, intimidation and economic boycotting.[26]

The process of redrawing boundaries according to ethnicity has generated significant disagreement and antagonism. Ethnic claims over minerals, lands, and water will continue to be explosive issues. In some cases where peoples of different ethnicities have coexisted peacefully for many generations, de facto ethnic segregation has proven a painful and difficult process. In other cases, long-standing ethnic tensions have been exacerbated by the forcible removal of people from lands that their families have tilled for generations. In yet other areas, tensions have been reduced because of increased commerce and access to decision-making structures. Minorities in some locations have at times claimed to be completely marginalized; in other areas, however, zonal administrations have allowed minorities to exercise control over language, education, culture, and village councils.

In nearly all areas, though, local administrators are ultimately answerable to the EPRDF, which maintains a high-level civilian official in each region alongside government forces to oversee policy decisions.

THE TIME DIMENSION IN PEACEBUILDING: THE CASE OF RWANDA

Peacebuilding, as Lederach emphasizes, is a complex enterprise, one involving a multiplicity of actors and activities pursuing a variety of overlapping objectives and operating within a variety of overlapping time frames. To help visualize the relationship between time frames and types of peacebuilding activities—and, in particular, to underline the need to harmonize immediate crisis responses with longer-term goals—Lederach presents a nested paradigm that models the time dimension in peacebuilding (see figure 6, page 77). This nested paradigm divides the time dimension into four phases, each of which is characterized by a particular category of peacebuilding activity: immediate action/crisis intervention; short-range planning/preparation and training; decade thinking/design of social change; and generational vision/desired future.

Rwanda provides an important series of lessons on how external do-gooders can inadvertently exacerbate the long-term dynamics of a situation by ill-timed and ill-conceived responses to a crisis.[27] Following the genocide in Rwanda in 1994 in which well over a half million people were killed, instability has been fostered by ex-army and militia elements associated with the genocidal regime through cross-border incursions into Zaire (now Congo), as well as by intimidation and massacres inside Rwanda when the bulk of the Rwandan refugees returned from Zaire in late 1996. The Rwandan government, composed of ex-rebels who defeated the regime that committed the genocide, is drawn largely from the Tutsi minority and faces multiple challenges.

In the following application of Lederach's framework to the Rwandan case, the case material focuses on the immediate aftermath of the genocide and the two-and-one-half-year period between the genocide and the time of this writing.

Immediate Action/Crisis Intervention

In April 1994, a genocide commenced in Rwanda in which the state organized and implemented the slaughter of thousands of people per day. In response, the rebel Rwandese Patriotic Front (RPF) began its offensive from its Ugandan base, causing hundreds of thousands of Hutus to flee the country over the borders into Zaire, Tanzania, and Burundi, largely under the control of the genocide organizers. Thus, stabilizing the situation required accomplishing two principal tasks: stopping the killing and meeting the needs of the refugees. As the international community quibbled over whether an outside force should be sent in, the RPF advanced through the country, routing the troops of the genocidal regime and taking Kigali in only a few short months. The RPF victory ended the genocide inside Rwanda. Another crisis emerged in the refugee camps in Zaire, when cholera spread like wildfire and killed thousands.

After responding impotently to the genocide, donor countries and agencies focused nearly all of their attention on the refugee camps, providing millions of dollars in military logistics to support a massive relief infrastructure, while virtually ignoring the rehabilitation needs inside Rwanda. Furthermore, although the humanitarian response was instrumental in preventing higher mortality rates in the refugee camps, the United Nations, the OAU, donor countries, and aid agencies were unable or unwilling to address the issue of separating refugees from the organizers of the genocide and armed elements of the former Rwandan army and their associated militias, particularly Interahamwe. In the absence of the political will to address the crisis, humanitarian agencies furnished aid that, though it saved lives, reinforced the authority structures of the perpetrators of genocide. In short, the immediate response to the genocide and resultant refugee crisis was an unmitigated disaster.

Short-Range Planning/Preparation and Training

In the short run, one of the most critical issues facing the newly constituted government in Rwanda was to break the cycle of impunity that had plagued the country since independence. To this end, the United Nations established a war crimes tribunal for the leading organizers of the genocide, and the Rwandan government began in 1996 to hold its own genocide trials for midlevel *genocidaires*.[28]

Most of the attention and much of the resources have gone to the International War Crimes Tribunal for Rwanda, which is based in Tanzania and has jurisdiction over the indictment of those responsible for the 1994 Rwandan genocide. Only a handful of people have been indicted, and many have not been delivered to the tribunal. The tribunal—predictably—is constrained by a lack of resources and authority in pursuing suspects. Arrested suspects include Theoneste Bagasora, one of the architects of the genocide, and Ferdinand Nahimana, owner of the infamous radio station Milles Collines, whose broadcasts helped facilitate the efficient execution of the genocide plan.

Delays in indictments, arrests, extradition, and prosecution have allowed both those who are guilty and those bent on vengeance time to regroup for further violence. The accused have jumped borders, seeking asylum abroad. Others—such as Major General Augustin Bizimungu, the former regime's military commander—escaped to Zaire and openly organized former Rwandan military and militia in the refugee camps. The whereabouts of many of the planners and leaders of the Rwandan genocide, as well as journalists responsible for hate media, remain largely unknown. Although the international community responded to the Rwandan request for an international tribunal, there has been little sustained, meaningful engagement of the United Nations to ensure that it accelerates its work.[29]

One suggestion to address the backlog in indictments and cases in the Rwandan Tribunal is to establish a truth commission to operate in tandem with the tribunal. Justice would be served with regard to the organizers of the genocide; others who participated would be named and their crimes exposed.

The success or failure of the international tribunal in Rwanda will have a significant impact on any eventual peace process, as the Rwandan government maintains its policy of "no reconciliation until justice." Meanwhile, the Rwandan government's own genocide trials are moving forward more rapidly, although many of the accused claim that they are being denied due process.

It is the national-level trials where Lederach's "Preparation and Training" phase is relevant to Rwanda. The Rwandan government has moved forward vigorously with hundreds of trials. This has required rapid interventions in the judicial sector, as dozens of Rwandans have been trained in all areas of criminal investigation, law, and penal administration. The preparation and training in which Rwanda is engaged to rebuild its society after the genocide are most pronounced in the national justice sector. Despite the higher visibility of, and better funding for, the international tribunal, Rwanda's commitment to rebuilding a functioning judiciary will be an equally important undertaking.

Decade Thinking/Design of Social Change

Social change is an overriding objective at this phase. The hatreds and divisions that parallel the fault lines within Rwandese society must be addressed through innovative programming in which external intervenors support local agents in the rebuilding of a healthier social capital. A variety of programs have already been initiated, including psychosocial interventions, reconciliation or social healing workshops, conflict management training, positive media programming, peace committees, and curriculum reform. The impact of these programs— examples of which follow—will not be apparent for five to ten years.

- Soon after the Rwandan genocide, it became apparent that orphaned or abandoned children were being warehoused, and the trauma of what had preceded their arrival was being compounded by the horrible conditions of their new setting. A few agencies responded to these conditions in the refugee camps and inside Rwanda by providing, among other services, counseling to the children. Save the Children–U.S. placed community youth workers within the centers in which the children were residing. In Kigali, support was given to local forms of social organization, such as scouts, traditional dance groups, soccer teams, and church groups. Community discussions were held about the future of the children. "Culture is the only thing big enough to help," asserted the director of one U.S. NGO in the aftermath of the genocide.[30] Africa Humanitarian Action, an Ethiopian-based organization, provides psychosocial trauma management, especially to Rwandese women. In addition, UNICEF has conducted seminars and training sessions in psychosocial trauma care.

  Soon after these agencies established modest psychosocial programs, dozens of NGOs followed suit. Despite little familiarity with local culture and conditions, many of these NGOs assumed that vast numbers of Rwandans were suffering from traumatization and launched a large number of psychosocial programs. Western diagnostic systems and treatments were applied, despite having little relevance to the realities of Rwandan life. Much of the distress that was diagnosed as trauma was, in fact, evidence of normal coping mechanisms in operation.[31] Furthermore, according to a multidonor evaluation, interventions aimed at traumatized children in unaccompanied minors' centers were not employing standardized criteria and practices, and suffered from little monitoring and follow-up.[32] (In Nicaragua, too, post-traumatic stress disorder diagnoses proved not to be reliable indicators of the need for psychological treatment.)[33] In fact, a review of the interviews and data from PTSD studies in Rwanda shows that very high percentages of people were not sad, were interested in work and play, and felt able to protect their families and themselves. By focusing solely on PTSD responses, NGOs and other intervenors are likely to address only the victimization and wounds of affected individuals, and to ignore their resilience. Such an approach reinforces the passivity of the "victim" and the knowledge of the "expert."[34] Encouragingly, however, lessons are being learned in the field and programming is being adjusted accordingly.

• A number of organizations are organizing social healing workshops. For example, Catholic Relief Services (CRS) and Kanyarwanda— a Rwandan human rights organization—sponsored a conference on reconciliation in Gisenyi, Rwanda. Held on September 22–25, 1995, the conference brought together sixteen members of Rwanda's government and civil society, and was moderated by Hizkias Assefa of the Nairobi Peace Initiative. The conference convened morally influential people to discuss strategies for reestablishing trust and confidence between Rwandan communities. Their conclusions underlined the importance of developing a culture that speaks the truth; the need to rehabilitate Rwandan society; recognition of justice as critical for Rwanda's recovery; the need to remove impediments to the return of refugees; and the need for a culture of sacrifice and goodwill. Following this meeting, CRS later sponsored a workshop organized by the Rwandan Association for Christian Workers, which involved church, media, and human rights and development groups in examining the role of the church and its justice and peace mission. CRS—like other agencies—continues to explore effective ways to build bridges between estranged communities.

The Rwandan government has also experimented with social healing workshops. For example, the Ministry of Higher Education conducted a seminar on tolerance in May 1995, broaching sensitive issues only a year after the genocide. "It provided an excellent opportunity to discuss serious issues," said a participant. "It gave the participants some space for reflection."[35]

- Conflict management training is another area in which a variety of agencies are seeking to establish indigenous mechanisms for sustainable processes of social change and conflict transformation. Africans for Humanitarian Action (AHA), an Ethiopian-run NGO, is undertaking capacity building in conflict management. AHA has conducted three workshops for government, civic groups, and agencies, in which participants have the opportunity to talk openly about the genocide. The participants in one of the sessions formed a contact group to pursue the topic of conflict resolution further; managing ethnic, cultural, and social differences was a major theme of their discussions.

- The radio was critical in Rwanda in mobilizing popular will and fostering a climate of fear and hatred that made the genocide possible. The government radio station in Zaire was partially responsible for fueling ethnic violence in Zaire in 1992–93 that uprooted half a million people. More broadly, the radio is a tool used by governments throughout Africa to perpetuate their power and justify their actions.

The United Nations High Commission on Refugees (UNHCR) undertook radio broadcasts in Rwanda and the refugee camps in neighboring Zaire and Tanzania that attempted to convince listeners that they could return safely to Rwanda. Similar messages were broadcast to refugees twice a week by Burundi national radio. UNICEF collaborated with the Rwandan Ministry of

Higher Education to produce a series of radio messages on cultural differences.

- Local variations on the peace committee concept are being tried. For example, the Committee for Restarting Pastoral Initiatives in Butare, Rwanda, led by a Tutsi priest and a Hutu intellectual, is receiving some support. The leaders are convinced that reconciliation must start at the grassroots. They issue a newsletter for public education purposes and are facilitating the return of refugees.

- Attitudinal change in the service of reconciliation objectives is a logical complement to educational policies at the primary and secondary level. Thus, developing training for teachers to help them encourage tolerance and cooperation among children is a cost-effective and comprehensive way to introduce reconciliation principles into the socialization process. Peace education programs are being explored by certain agencies, based in schools, communities, media, and religious institutions. One agency official proclaimed that in Rwanda, "there must be a massive education program to new ideas of inclusivity."[36] A major initiative by the Ministry of Higher Education is to train community leaders in primary and secondary schools. Planning is under way to introduce into the school curriculum peace education, a central theme of which would be how people and communities have overcome past differences and reintegrated.

Generational Vision/Desired Future

If enduring peace is ever to come to Rwanda, a series of structural issues must be addressed—even within the context of programming for action in the immediate and short-range time frames. The control of resources, and land tenure in particular, is a principal problem in Rwanda, the most densely populated country in Africa. There is tremendous competition over arable land among long-time residents, Tutsi returnees after the assumption of power by the RPF in 1994, and now Hutu returnees who came back in the hundreds of thousands as 1996 drew to a close. Addressing the resource conundrum will involve promoting a mixture of alternative livelihoods, diversification of sustainable agricultural and pastoral production, more stable export markets and prices, equal access to government agricultural training and inputs, dispute resolution mechanisms, population programming, low-cost housing, and common land use arrangements. The pursuit of each of these objectives is likely to involve not only officials of the Rwandan government but also community leaders and representatives of local and international NGOs, the World Bank, and other intergovernmental agencies—all of whom will have to directly factor peacebuilding objectives into their programming, rather than strictly adhering to efficiency and productivity goals.

Another issue that will have to be addressed is the method by which power is shared in the country. It is unrealistic to expect the victorious RPF government to bend over backward to share power with groups that will likely be infiltrated or controlled by genocide organizers. Nevertheless, Rwandan history has shown that exclusion of one group or another over an extended period of time is a recipe for disaster. The Rwandan government is attempting to entice qualified Hutus into government service and to diversify its armed forces by recruiting Hutu soldiers untainted by involvement in the genocide. Neither policy is likely to satisfy Hutu leaders in the long run. Thus, creative arrangements will have to be devised to reduce the likelihood of violence, such as the decentralization of administration and the devolution of political and economic decision making, as well as a means of sharing power at the national level.

A yet more challenging task is to find a regional solution to the problems posed by ill-drawn national borders. "Bad borders make bad neighbors," someone once remarked about Somalia, and the adage has relevance for the Great Lakes states as well: Burundi is prey to civil war; the future cohesion of the Congo is by no means assured; and Rwanda has a history scarred by massacres and genocide. Enlightened and sustained leadership from regional governments and organizations, international players, national actors, and local peace constituencies will be required if any progress toward a less contentious national demarcation of the Great Lakes region is to be achieved.

TRANSFORMATIVE APPROACHES TO TRAINING:
THE CASE OF SOMALIA

Lederach urges that instead of focusing on conflict resolution training as an "event" involving the "transfer of content," we adopt a more transformative approach. "A transformative approach," he writes, "suggests that training is less about the transfer of content than it is about the creation of a dynamic process involving key people who together focus on the realities of the conflict in their context" (page 109, above).

One of the richest examples of such an approach in the African context is the effort by Sweden's Life and Peace Institute to encourage the formation of district councils in Somalia and to train the councilors as a mechanism for institutionalizing long-term conflict prevention and management. The experiment—still ongoing—is one in which the intentions were and are consistent with Lederach's vision of transformative training; early problems of implementation, however, have hindered the success of the initiative.

The Life and Peace Institute (LPI) and the UN Operation in Somalia (UNOSOM) attempted to recreate civil administrative authority in a situation of state collapse by implementing the results of an agreement among warring Somali factions to allow the creation of district councils. The Addis Ababa peace agreement in March 1993 staked out a "two-track" approach to peace in Somalia, with peacemaking at the grassroots meant to parallel a process of accommodation among warlords. The district councils were envisioned as the lowest level of local administration in the reconstitution of the Somali state.

LPI established district council training centers in a number of locations throughout Somalia, with international trainers paired with Somali counterparts. District councilors undergo roughly a week of training in administration and management. Training sessions usually bring together council members from a number of different locations, stimulating cross-communal interchange and communication. As agreed by the factions present at the Addis Ababa conference, a woman must be on each district council.

The district councils are a new development in Somali political institution building and arguably allow a new approach to participation. They are nevertheless a foreign entity, whose structural blueprint—although endorsed by warlord negotiators—was determined externally, without the participation of the local community. In some places, the new form of participation may work, and communities may come to feel that they "own" their councils. But in other locations, parallel structures have already formed, and district councils have been marginalized and rejected as an external imposition. In still others, the councils threatened existing interests and have for that reason been sidelined.[37]

UNOSOM's hasty implementation of the concept of the district councils also undermined their validity. At the time of elections to the councils, in many areas so many people had been displaced that truly representative institutions could not be achieved. In other locations, district councils grossly overrepresent the locally dominant subclan, and training sessions for such councils arguably buttress the legitimacy of those imbalances.[38] Research by Mark Bradbury has identified other concerns, including the legitimacy of the districts; the extent of external manipulation of the council elections; the bureaucratic centralism of UNOSOM; the replacement of existing local governmental structures; the tokenism of the one-woman requirement; the uncertainty over council jurisdiction and authority; the lack of resources; the inadequate time allotted both for UNOSOM to form the councils and for councilors to be trained; and the uncertain role of elders in forming the councils.[39]

Of even greater import are concerns about the degree to which communities feel that they own these district councils. In Bay and Bakool (before the warlord Mohamed Farah Aidid's September 1995 invasion of Baidoa), the creation of a clan-based Supreme Council rendered the local district councils largely irrelevant, as did the resumption of elder authority in Absame areas of the Juba Valley. In these places, clan affinity is the primary mobilizing factor. In fact, where district councils do remain, they are being reoriented and reconstituted by the local authority structure. Elders continue to be the primary agents of conflict prevention and management.

Despite these problems, LPI's initiative has yielded some positive results. Training sessions have given councilors an opportunity to analyze the political, economic, and social environment of their communities; to explore the kinds of alternatives that might strengthen conflict prevention and management in their areas; and to recognize their potential role in implementing change. Even in the absence of the establishment of effective local administrative structures, hundreds of local community leaders throughout Somalia have received training that will enhance their own efforts to transform their local situation.

CONCLUSION

Lederach's contribution exposes the paucity of concerted peacebuilding efforts within the official diplomatic community, particularly those directed at the key middle-level actors. Since the early 1990s, donor government aid agencies—as well as NGOs—have begun to recognize this shortcoming, and more focused interventions in support of middle-level capacities for peace are being undertaken.

Northeast Africa offers a hopeful sign. The regional organization IGAD has made the prevention of conflict one of its organizational priorities and is attempting to build its capacity to carry out this mandate. In response, the U.S. government initiated the Greater Horn of Africa Initiative, which also prioritizes conflict prevention and which is attempting to better integrate peacebuilding strategies in this conflict-prone region. This provides an opening to operationalize many of the ideas contained in this volume.

In sum, the conceptual models provided by John Paul Lederach form an elaborate framework for deeper analysis into not only the causes of conflict but also the peacebuilding approaches that address these causes. With such an analytical framework in hand, policymakers will find it easier to develop a more rational policy process, international agencies will be better able to tailor their interventions to the needs of a given context, and diplomats will better appreciate the long-term requirements of conflict resolution.

NOTES

• • •

1. GLOBAL OVERVIEW

1. Sun Tzu, *The Art of War,* ed. and trans. Thomas Cleary (New York: Shambhala, 1991); Carl Von Clausewitz, *On War* (London: Penguin, 1978); Quincy Wright, *A Study of War* (Chicago: University of Chicago Press, 1942); and Richard Barnet, *Roots of War* (New York: Penguin, 1978).

2. Lewis Richardson, *Statistics of Deadly Quarrels* (Pittsburgh: Boxwood, 1960).

3. Johann Galtung, *Essays in Peace Research,* 5 vols. (Copenhagen: Ejlers, 1978); and Kenneth Boulding, *Conflict and Defense* (New York: Harper and Row, 1963).

4. See, for example, Ruth Leger Sivard, *World and Social Expenditures* (Washington, D.C.: World Priorities, 1983); Stockholm International Peace Research Institute Staff, *SIPRI Yearbook 1995: Armaments, Disarmament, and International Security* (Oxford: Oxford University Press, 1995); and Ernie Regehr, "Armed Conflict in the World in 1992," *Ploughshares Monitor* 13, no. 4 (December 1996): 13–17.

5. Peter Wallensteen and Karin Axell, "Armed Conflict at the End of the Cold War, 1989–1992," *Journal of Peace Research* 30, no. 3 (August 1993): 331–346.

6. Johann Galtung, "Peace Education: Problems and Conflicts," in *Education for Peace,* ed. M. Haavelsrud (Guildford, Conn.: Science and Technology Press, 1976), 80–87; and Tony Ives, "The Geography of Arms Dispersal," in David Pepper and Alan Jenkins, eds., *The Geography of Peace and War* (Oxford: Basil Blackwell, 1987).

7. Dayle Spencer, William Spencer, and William Ury, eds., *The State of the World Conflict Report* (Atlanta: International Negotiation Network of the Carter Center, 1992).

8. Johann Galtung, *The True Worlds: A Transnational Perspective* (New York: Free Press, 1980).

9. Sivard, *World and Social Expenditures;* and Ives, "Geography of Arms Dispersal," 42–49.

10. Ives, "Geography of Arms Dispersal," 44–45.

11. Peter Wallensteen, "Conflict Resolution after the Cold War: Five Implications," in Honggang Yang, ed., *Resolving Intra-National Conflicts: A Strengthened Role for Intergovernmental Organizations,* Conference Report Series, vol. 5, no. 1 (Atlanta: Carter Center, 1993), 34–42.

12. See, for example, John Mueller, *Retreat from Doomsday: The Obsolescence of Major War* (New York: Basic, 1989).

13. See, for example, John J. Mearsheimer, "Back to the Future: Instability in Europe after the Cold War," *International Security* 15, no. 1 (summer 1990): 5–56.

14. Ernie Regehr, *War after the Cold War: Shaping a Canadian Response,* Ploughshares Working Paper 93-3 (Waterloo, Ontario: Project Ploughshares, 1993).

15. Regehr, "Armed Conflict in the World in 1992," 16.

16. Mats Friberg, "The Need for Unofficial Diplomacy in Identity Conflicts," in Tonci Kuzmanic and Arno Truger, eds., *Yugoslavia Wars* (Ljubljana, Slovenia: Peace Institute, 1992), 62.

17. Regehr, *War after the Cold War.*

18. Wallensteen and Axell, "Armed Conflict at the End of the Cold War," 334.

2. CHARACTERISTICS OF DEEPLY DIVIDED SOCIETIES

1. Manus I. Midlarsky, *The Internationalization of Communal Strife* (New York: Routledge, 1992).

2. James Coleman, *Community Conflict* (New York: Free Press, 1956); and Lewis Coser, *The Functions of Social Conflict* (New York: Free Press, 1956).

3. Wallensteen and Axell, "Armed Conflict at the End of the Cold War," 334.

4. Suzanne Lunden, *The Horn of Africa Bulletin* (Uppsala, Sweden: Life and Peace Institute, 1993).

5. Kumar Ruppesinghe, *Conflict Transformation* (London: Macmillan, 1994), 65.

6. Louis Kriesberg, *Intractable Conflicts and Their Transformation* (Syracuse: Syracuse University Press, 1989), 5.

7. Herbert Kelman, *International Behavior: A Social-Psychological Analysis* (New York: Holt, Rinehart and Winston, 1965); and Vamik Volkan, Demetrios Julius, and Joseph Montville, *The Psychodynamics of International Relations* (Lexington, Mass.: Lexington, 1990).

8. Coleman, *Community Conflict.*

9. Dayle Spencer and William Spencer, *The International Negotiation Network: A New Method of Approaching Some Very Old Problems,* Carter Center Occasional Paper Series, vol. 2, no. 2 (Atlanta: Carter Center, 1992).

PART II, INTRODUCTION

1. John Paul Lederach, "Conflict Transformation: The Case for Peace Advocacy," in Menno Wiebe, ed., *NGOs and Peacemaking: A Prospect for the Horn* (Waterloo, Ontario: Conrad Grebel College, 1989).

3. RECONCILIATION

1. Hizkias Assefa, *Peace and Reconciliation as a Paradigm* (Nairobi, Kenya: Nairobi Peace Initiative), 10–16; and Howard Zehr, *Changing Lanes: New Perspectives in Crime and Punishment* (Scottdale, Pa.: Herald Press, 1990), 177.

2. Harold H. Saunders, *The Concept of Relationship* (Columbus: Ohio State University, Mershon Center, 1993); and Joseph Montville, *Conflict and Peacemaking in Multi-Ethnic Societies* (Lexington, Mass.: Lexington, 1990).

3. Harold H. Saunders and Randa Slim, "Dialogue to Change Conflictual Relationships," *Higher Education Exchange* (a Kettering newsletter) (1994): 43–56.

4. Margaret J. Wheatley, *Leadership and the New Science* (San Francisco: Berrett-Koehler, 1992).

5. Assefa, *Peace and Reconciliation.*

6. John Paul Lederach, *The Journey toward Reconciliation* (Scottdale, Pa.: Herald Press, in press).

7. Kenwin K. Smith and David N. Berg, *Paradoxes of Group Life* (San Francisco: Jossey-Bass, 1987).

8. Ibid., 25.

9. Gerald Shenk, *God with Us? The Role of Religion in Conflicts in the Former Yugoslavia,* Research Report no. 15 (Uppsala, Sweden: Life and Peace Institute, 1993).

10. See, for example, John Burton, *Resolving Deep-Rooted Conflict: A Handbook* (Lanham, Md.: University Press of America, 1987); R. J. Fisher, "Conflict Analysis Workshop on Cyprus: Final Workshop Report" (Canadian Institute for International Peace and Security, Ottawa, 1991); and Jay Rothman, *From Confrontation to Cooperation* (London: Sage, 1992).

11. Jane Corbin, *The Norway Channel: The Secret Talks That Led to the Middle East Peace Accord* (New York: Atlantic Monthly Press, 1994).

12. Corbin, *Norway Channel;* and Amos Elon, "The Peacemakers," *New Yorker,* 20 December 1993, 77–85.

13. Elon, "Peacemakers," 80.

14. Corbin, *Norway Channel,* 50.

15. Elon, "Peacemakers," 81.

16. Ibid., 82.

17. Ibid.

4. STRUCTURE

1. Michael Parenti, *Inventing Reality: The Politics of the Mass Media* (New York: St. Martin's, 1990).

2. Roger Fisher and William Ury, *Getting to Yes* (Boston: Houghton Mifflin, 1981), 3.

3. John Burton, *Conflict and Communication* (London: Macmillan, 1969); and Burton, *Resolving Deep-Rooted Conflict.*

4. Herbert Kelman, "Creating the Conditions for Israeli-Palestinian Negotiations," *Journal of Conflict Resolution* 26 (1982): 39–75.

5. Ronald Fisher, *Interactive Conflict Resolution* (Syracuse: Syracuse University Press, 1997), 7.

6. M. H. Banks and Christopher Mitchell, *Handbook of Conflict Resolution: The Analytical Problem-Solving Approach* (London: Pinter, 1996).

7. Christopher Mitchell, "External Peace-Making Initiatives and Intranational Conflict," in Manus I. Midlarsky, ed., *The Internationalization of Communal Strife* (New York: Routledge, 1992), 75.

8. Beatrice Schultz, "Conflict Resolution Training Programs: Implications for Theory and Research," *Negotiation Journal* 5, no. 3 (1989): 301–309.

9. John Paul Lederach, *Preparing for Peace: Conflict Transformation across Cultures* (Syracuse: Syracuse University Press, 1995).

10. Ron Kraybill, interview by author, June 16, 1994.

11. Paula Gutlove and Joe Montville, "Toward Sustainable Peace in the Balkans" (unpublished report, Balkans Peace Project, Cambridge, Mass., 1992).

12. Mari Fitzduff, *Beyond Violence: Conflict Resolution Processes in Northern Ireland* (Tokyo: United Nations University, 1996).

13. Assefa, *Peace and Reconciliation;* and Harold Miller, *Peace and Reconciliation in Africa,* Mennonite Central Committee Occasional Paper no. 19 (Akron, Pa.: Mennonite Central Committee, July 1993).

14. "Peace and Reconciliation in Angola and Mozambique" (communiqué from participants in Lusophone Consultation, Limuru, Kenya, 20–27 September, 1990).

15. Jack Child, *The Central American Peace Process, 1983–1991* (Boulder, Colo.: Lynne Rienner, 1992).

16. Paul Wehr and John Paul Lederach, "Mediating Conflict in Central America," *Journal of Peace Research* 28, no. 1 (February 1991): 85–98.

17. Bruce Nichols, "Religious Conciliation between the Sandinistas and the East Coast Indians of Nicaragua," in Doug Johnston and Cynthia Sampson, eds., *Religion: The Missing Dimension in Statecraft* (Oxford: Oxford University Press, 1994).

18. Wehr and Lederach, "Mediating Conflict," 97.

19. Laurie Nathan, "An Imperfect Bridge: Crossing to Democracy on the Peace Accord," *Track Two* 2 (May 1993).

20. Prioshaw Camay, "The JOCC Solution," *Track Two* 2, no. 4 (November 1993): 16–17.

21. Ed Garcia, *Participative Approaches to Peacemaking in the Philippines* (Tokyo: United Nations University, 1993).

22. John Paul Lederach, "Tapping the Tradition: Cultural Elements of the Peace Process in Somalia" (paper presented at the National Conference of Peacemaking and Conflict Resolution, Portland, Ore., May 1993), 8.

23. Ahmed Yusef Farah, *The Roots of Reconciliation* (London: Action Aid, 1993).

24. Alta Brubaker, "Preparing People for Peace" (report no. 4 of the Program of Work by the Peace and Reconciliation Committee of the Christian Council of Mozambique, Nampula, Mozambique, 1993), 4.

25. Barbara Kolucki, *Circo da Paz* (New York: UNICEF, 1993).

26. Barry Hart, interview by author, Harrisonburg, Virginia, June 1993.

27. Maire Dugan, "A Nested Theory of Conflict," *Women in Leadership* 1, no. 1 (summer 1996): 9–20.

28. Roland Marchal, "Formes de la violence dans un espace urbain en guerre: Les Mooryaan de Mogadiscio," *Cahiers d'études Africaines* 117 (October 1993).

29. John Paul Lederach, "Proposal for a Disarmament and Rehabilitation Pilot Project" (paper submitted to the Life and Peace Institute and UNOSOM, Uppsala, Sweden, 17 November 1992).

30. Ernie Regehr, "Report on the Disarmament Resource Group" (working group report, Frankfurt, December 1993).

5. PROCESS

1. Louis Kriesberg, *The Sociology of Social Conflict* (Englewood Cliffs, N.J.: Prentice-Hall, 1973), 4.

2. John Paul Lederach, "Conflict Transformation: The Case for Peace Advocacy," in Menno Wiebe, ed., *NGOs and Peacemaking: A Prospect for the Horn* (Waterloo, Ontario: Conrad Grebel College, 1989).

3. Adam Curle, *Making Peace* (London: Tavistock, 1971).

4. James Laue and Gerald Cormick, "The Ethics of Intervention in Community Disputes," in Gordon Bermant, Herbert C. Kelman, and Donald P. Warwick, eds., *The Ethics of Social Intervention* (Washington, D.C.: Halsted Press, 1978), 212.

5. Mitchell, "External Peace-Making Initiatives."

6. Ibid., 147.

7. Louis Kriesberg, "Formal and Quasi-Mediators in International Disputes: An Exploratory Analysis," *Journal of Peace Research* 28, no. 1 (February 1991): 19–27.

8. Loraleigh Keashley and Ronald Fisher, "Toward a Contingency Approach to Third-Party Intervention in Regional Conflict: A Cyprus Illustration," *International Journal* 45 (spring 1990): 424–453.

9. Mitchell, "External Peace-Making Initiatives," 140.

6. AN INTEGRATED FRAMEWORK FOR PEACEBUILDING

1. Regehr, *War after the Cold War*, 1.

2. See John Paul Lederach, "The Ethics of Military Intervention in Humanitarian Crises," in United Nations Development Programme, *UNDP Training Manual* (New York: United Nations, 1993), 2.

3. Ann Seidman and Anang Frederick, *Towards a New Vision of Self-Sustained Development* (Trenton, N.J.: Africa World Press, 1992); Michael Carley and Ian Christie, *Managing Sustainable Development* (Minneapolis: University of Minnesota Press, 1992); and Julie Fisher, *The Road from Rio: Sustainable Development and the Nongovernmental Movement in the Third World* (New York: Praeger, 1993).

4. Elise Boulding, "The Challenges of Imaging Peace in Wartime," *Futures* 23, no. 5 (1991): 528.

5. Lederach, *Journey toward Reconciliation* (see the chapter on time, healing, and reconciliation).

6. Christopher W. Moore, *Dispute Management Systems Design* (Boulder, Colo.: LDR Associates, 1994).

7. Wheatley, *Leadership and the New Sciences,* 15.

7. RESOURCES

1. Robert Merton, *Social Theory and Social Structure* (Glencoe, Ill.: Free Press, 1965).

2. Mary Anderson, *Do No Harm: Supporting Local Capacities for Peace through Aid* (Cambridge, Mass.: Development of Collaborative Action, Inc., 1996).

3. Lederach, *Preparing for Peace.*

4. Farah, *Roots of Reconciliation.*

5. Kolucki, *Circo da Paz.*

6. John Paul Lederach, "Transformation from Within: Peacemaking in the East Coast of Nicaragua" (paper commissioned by George Fox College under a grant from the United States Institute of Peace, 1989).

7. Wehr and Lederach, "Mediating Conflict," 97.

8. COORDINATION

1. Mari Fitzduff, *Beyond Violence: Conflict Resolution Processes in Northern Ireland* (Tokyo: United Nations University, 1996), chapter 9.

2. Louise Diamond and John McDonald, *Multi-Track Diplomacy: A Systems Approach to Peace,* 3d. ed. (West Hartford, Conn.: Kumarian Press, 1995).

3. Lunden, *Horn of Africa Bulletin.*

4. Suzanne Lunden, "Working Document of the Life and Peace Institute on Somalia" (Life and Peace Institute, Uppsala, Sweden, 1992), 14.

5. Sture Normark, Suzanne Lunden, and John Paul Lederach, "Blueprint: Somali Reconciliation Structure," working paper, Life and Peace Institute, Uppsala, Sweden, 3.

6. Wolfgang Heinrich, "Report on the Life and Peace Institute's Somali Initiative" (Life and Peace Institute, Uppsala, Sweden, 1996).

9. PREPARING FOR PEACEBUILDING

1. Lederach, *Preparing for Peace*, chap. 1.

2. Ibid., 21.

3. Ibid., chaps. 5 and 6.

4. Juan Gutierrez, *The Horizon of Reconciliation* (Gernika, Spain: Red Gernika, in press).

10. STRATEGIC AND RESPONSIVE EVALUATION

1. My working paper, prepared for the Organization of American State's PROPAZ Guatemala project, was entitled "Peacebuilding in Divided Societies: Tools for Strategic and Responsive Evaluation"; it was issued in January 1997.

2. Ed Hall, *The Dance of Life: The Other Dimension of Time* (New York: Doubleday, 1984), chap. 3.

3. Jay Rothman, "Action Evaluation: Draft Discussion Paper" (paper presented as part of a Pew Foundation research paper, March 1996).

4. Carol Weiss, "Nothing as Practical as a Good Theory: Exploring Theory-Based Evaluation for Comprehensive Community Initiatives for Children and Families," in James P. Connell et al., eds., *New Approaches to Evaluating Community Initiatives* (Washington, D.C.: Aspen Institute, 1995), 65–93.

5. Joyce Hocker and William Wilmot, *Interpersonal Conflict* (Madison, Wis.: Brown and Benchmark, 1995), 57–63.

APPLYING CONCEPTS TO CASES

1. For more, see John Prendergast, *The Outcry for Peace in the Sudan* (Washington, D.C.: Center for Strategic Initiatives of Women, October 1996).

2. See John Prendergast, *Crisis Response: Humanitarian Band-Aids in Sudan and Somalia* (London: Pluto Press, 1997), chap. 3.

3. N. Richman, "Annotation: Children in Situations of Political Violence," *Journal of Child Psychology and Psychiatry* 34 (1995): 1286–1302.

4. Everett Ressler, *Children in War* (New York: UNICEF, 1991), 181.

5. John Prendergast, *Dare to Hope: Children of War in Southern Sudan*, Center of Concern Advocacy Paper (Washington, D.C.: Center of Concern, 1996).

6. Julia Aker Duany, "Making Peace: A Report on Grassroots Peace Efforts" (Union Institute, October 1995, unpublished mimeograph), 19.

7. William Lowrey, "The Role of Religion in Peacemaking and Reconciliation: A Case Study among the Nuer in Sudan" (Union Institute, unpublished mimeograph), 9.

8. Duany, "Making Peace," 6.

9. Interview by author, southern Sudan, July 10, 1995.

10. UNICEF, *Children and Women in Ethiopia* (Addis Ababa: UNICEF, 1993), 24.

11. Raymond Copson, *Africa's Wars and Prospects for Peace* (New York: M. E. Sharpe, 1994), 90.

12. Interview by author, Addis Ababa, October 3, 1995.

13. John Markakis, "Ethnic Conflict and the State in the Horn of Africa," in Katsuyo Fukui and John Markakis, *Ethnicity and Conflict in the Horn of Africa* (London: James Currey, 1994), 235.

14. The following comes largely from John Prendergast, *Governance, Political Islam, and Conflict in Ethiopia* (Washington, D.C.: Center for Strategic Initiatives of Women, forthcoming).

15. Kuawab Business Consultants, "Fertilizer Marketing Survey: Main Recommendations," report for USAID/Ethiopia, October 1995.

16. Robert Shank, "1996 Fertilizer Situation: Progress, Problems, and Programs" (UN Emergencies Unit for Ethiopia, Addis Ababa, September 1996), 2.

17. Shank, "1996 Fertilizer Situation," 1, 3.

18. Ben Parker, *Ethiopia: Breaking New Ground* (Oxford: Oxfam, 1995), 35.

19. Interview by author, Addis Ababa, November 3, 1996.

20. Jon Abbink, "Breaking and Making the State: The Dynamics of Ethnic Democracy in Ethiopia," *Journal of Contemporary African Studies* 13, no. 2 (1996): 156.

21. National Democratic Institute, *An Evaluation of the June 21 Ethiopian Elections in Ethiopia* (Washington, D.C.: National Democratic Institute, 1992); and International Human Rights Law Group, *Ethiopia in Transition: A Report on the Judiciary and the Legal Profession* (Washington, D.C.: International Human Rights Law Group, 1994).

22. John Cohen, "Decentralization and 'Ethnic Federalism' in Post–Civil War Ethiopia," in Krishna Kumar, ed., *Rebuilding Societies after Civil War: Critical Roles for International Assistance* (Boulder, Colo.: Lynne Rienner, 1996), 141.

23. Economist Intelligence Unit, *Ethiopia Country Report: Second Quarter 1996* (London: Economist Intelligence Unit, May 1996), 5.

24. World Bank, *Ethiopia: Public Expenditure Review—Issues in Public Expenditure* (Washington, D.C.: World Bank, 1995).

25. Satish Chandra Mirsha, "The Economic Dimensions of Regionalization in Ethiopia" (USAID report, Nairobi, 1995); and Cohen, "Decentralization and 'Ethnic Federalism,'" 146.

26. Abbink, "Breaking and Making the State," 153.

27. See John Prendergast, *Frontline Diplomacy: Humanitarian Aid and Conflict in Africa* (Boulder, Colo.: Lynne Rienner, 1996), chap. 2.

28. For more on war tribunals, see John Prendergast, Jennifer Ragland, and Renee Storteboom, "Post-Conflict Reconciliation Initiatives: Preliminary Observations" (USAID/CDIE report, Washington, D.C., 1996).

29. African Centre for the Constructive Resolution of Disputes (ACCORD), *State, Sovereignty, and Responsibility* [papers from the African Conference on Peacemaking and Conflict Resolution] (Durban, South Africa: ACCORD, 1996), 71.

30. Interview by author, Kigali, August 8, 1995.

31. Derek Summerfield, *The Impact of War and Atrocity on Civilian Populations,* Relief and Rehabilitation Network paper no. 4 (London: Overseas Development Institute, April 1996), 15–16.

32. See Krishna Kumar, ed., *Rebuilding Societies after Civil War: Critical Roles for International Assistance* (Boulder, Colo.: Lynne Rienner, 1996), 65.

33. F. Hume and D. Summerfield, "After the War in Nicaragua: A Psychosocial Study of War Wounded Ex-Combatants," *Medicine and War* 10 (1991): 4–25.

34. Summerfield, *Impact of War and Atrocity,* 16–17.

35. Interview by author, Kigali, August 4, 1995.

36. Interview by author, Kigali, August 6, 1995.

37. Ken Menkhaus and John Prendergast, "The Political Economy of Post-Intervention Somalia," *CSIS Africa Notes,* no. 172 (May 1995).

38. See Prendergast, *Frontline Diplomacy*; and David R. Smock, ed., *Creative Approaches to Managing Conflict in Africa: Findings from USIP-Funded Projects,* Peaceworks no. 15 (Washington, D.C.: United States Institute of Peace Press, April 1997).

39. Mark Bradbury, *The Somali Conflict: Prospects for Peace,* Oxfam Research Paper no. 9 (Oxford: Oxfam, 1994), 4.

BIBLIOGRAPHY

● ● ●

Anderson, Mary. *Do No Harm: Supporting Local Capacities for Peace through Aid.* Cambridge, Mass.: Development for Collaborative Action, Inc., 1996.

Assefa, Hizkias. "Humanitarian Activity and Peacemaking: Challenge for the NGOs." Nairobi, Kenya, 15 May 1991. Mimeographed.

———. *Peace and Reconciliation as a Paradigm.* Nairobi, Kenya: Nairobi Peace Initiative, 1993.

Banks, M. H., and Christopher Mitchell. *Handbook of Conflict Resolution: The Analytical Problem-Solving Approach.* London: Pinter, 1996.

Barnet, Richard. *Roots of War.* New York: Penguin, 1978.

Boulding, Elise. "The Challenges of Imaging Peace in Wartime." *Futures* 23, no. 5 (1991).

Boulding, Kenneth. *Conflict and Defense.* New York: Harper and Row, 1963.

Boutros-Ghali, Boutros. *An Agenda for Peace.* New York: United Nations, 1992.

Brubaker, Alta. "Preparing People for Peace." Report no. 4 of the Program of Work by the Peace and Reconciliation Committee of the Christian Council of Mozambique. Nampula, Mozambique, 1993.

Burton, John. *Conflict and Communication.* London: Macmillan, 1969.

———. *Resolving Deep-Rooted Conflict: A Handbook.* Lanham, Md.: University Press of America, 1987.

Camay, Prioshaw. "The JOCC Solution." *Track Two* 2, no. 4 (November 1993): 16–17.

Carley, Michael, and Ian Christie. *Managing Sustainable Development.* Minneapolis: University of Minnesota Press, 1992.

Child, Jack. *The Central American Peace Process 1983–1991*. Boulder, Colo.: Lynne Rienner, 1992.

Clausewitz, Carl Von. *On War*. London: Penguin, 1978.

Coleman, James. *Community Conflict*. New York: Free Press, 1956.

Corbin, Jane. The *Norway Channel: The Secret Talks That Led to the Middle East Peace Accord*. New York: Atlantic Monthly Press, 1994.

Coser, Lewis. *The Functions of Social Conflict*. New York: Free Press, 1956.

Curle, Adam. *Making Peace*. London: Tavistock, 1971.

———. *Tools for Transformation*. London: Hawthorn Press, 1990.

Diamond, Louise, and John McDonald. *Multi-Track Diplomacy: A Systems Approach to Peace*, 3d ed. West Hartford, Conn.: Kumarian Press, 1995.

Dugan, Maire. "A Nested Theory of Conflict." *Women in Leadership* 1, no. 1 (summer 1996): 9–20.

Elon, Amos. "The Peacemakers." *New Yorker*, 20 December 1993, 77–85.

Farah, Ahmed Yusef. *The Roots of Reconciliation*. London: Action Aid, 1993.

Fisher, Julie. *The Road from Rio: Sustainable Development and the Non-governmental Movement in the Third World*. New York: Praeger, 1993.

Fisher, Roger, and William Ury. *Getting to Yes*. Boston: Houghton Mifflin, 1981.

Fisher, Ronald. "Conflict Analysis Workshop on Cyprus: Final Workshop Report." Ottawa, Canadian Institute for International Peace and Security, 1991.

———. *Interactive Conflict Resolution*. Syracuse: Syracuse University Press, 1997.

———. "Third Party Consultation as a Method of Conflict Resolution: A Review of Studies." *Journal of Conflict Resolution* 27 (1983): 301–334.

Fitzduff, Mari. *Beyond Violence: Conflict Resolution Processes in Northern Ireland*. Tokyo: United Nations University, 1996.

Friberg, Mats. "The Need for Unofficial Diplomacy in Identity Conflicts." In *Yugoslavia Wars*, edited by Tonci Kuzmanic and Arno Truger. Ljubljana, Slovenia: Peace Institute, 1992.

Galtung, Johann. *Essays in Peace Research*. 5 vols. Copenhagen: Ejlers, 1978.

———. "Peace Education: Problems and Conflicts." In *Education for Peace*, edited by M. Haavelsrud. Guildford, Conn.: Science and Technology Press, 1976.

———. *The True Worlds: A Transactive Perspective*. New York: Free Press, 1980.

Garcia, Ed. *Participative Approaches to Peacemaking in the Philippines.* Tokyo: United Nations University, 1993.

Gutierrez, Juan. *The Horizon of Reconciliation.* Gernika, Spain: Red Gernika, in press.

Gutlove, Paula, and Joe Montville. "Toward Sustainable Peace in the Balkans." Balkans Peace Project, Cambridge, Mass., 1992.

Heinrich, Wolfgang. "Report on the Life and Peace Institute's Somali Initiative." Uppsala, Sweden: Life and Peace Institute, 1996.

Hocker, Joyce, and William Wilmot. *Interpersonal Conflict.* Madison, Wis.: Brown and Benchmark, 1995.

Ives, Tony. "The Geography of Arms Dispersal." In *The Geography of Peace of War,* edited by David Pepper and Alan Jenkins. Oxford: Basil Blackwell, 1987.

Keashley, Loraleigh, and Ronald Fisher. "Towards a Contingency Approach to Third Party Intervention in Regional Conflict: A Cyprus Illustration." *International Journal* 45 (spring 1990): 424–453.

Kelman, Herbert. *International Behavior: A Social-Psychological Analysis.* New York: Holt, Rinehart, and Winston, 1965.

———. "Creating the Conditions for Israeli-Palestinian Negotiations." *Journal of Conflict Resolution* 26 (1982): 39–75.

Kolucki, Barbara. *Circo da Paz.* New York: UNICEF, 1993.

Kriesberg, Louis. "Formal and Quasi-Mediators in International Disputes: An Exploratory Analysis." *Journal of Peace Research* 28, no. 1 (February 1991): 19–27.

———. *Intractable Conflicts and Their Transformation.* Syracuse: Syracuse University Press, 1989.

———. *The Sociology of Social Conflict.* Englewood Cliffs, N.J.: Prentice Hall, 1973.

Laue, James, and Gerald Cormick. "The Ethics of Intervention in Community Disputes." In *The Ethics of Social Intervention,* edited by Gordon Bermant, Herbert C. Kelman, and Donald P. Warwick. Washington, D.C.: Halsted Press, 1978.

Lederach, John Paul. "Beyond Violence: Building Sustainable Peace." In *Beyond Violence,* edited by Arthur Williamson. Belfast: Community Relations Council, 1995.

———. "Conflict Transformation: The Case for Peace Advocacy." In *NGOs and Peacemaking: A Prospect for the Horn,* edited by Menno Wiebe. Waterloo, Ontario: Conrad Grebel College, 1989.

———. "The Ethics of Military Intervention in Humanitarian Crises." In *UNDP Training Manual*. New York: United Nations, 1993.

———. *The Journey toward Reconciliation*. Scottdale, Pa.: Herald Press, in press.

———. *Preparing for Peace: Conflict Transformation across Cultures*. Syracuse: Syracuse University Press, 1995.

———. "Proposal for a Disarmament and Rehabilitation Pilot Project." Paper submitted to the Life and Peace Institute and UNOSOM, Uppsala, Sweden, 17 November 1992.

———. "Tapping the Tradition: Cultural Elements of the Peace Process in Somalia." Paper presented at the National Conference of Peacemaking and Conflict Resolution, Portland, Ore., May 1993.

———. "Transformation from Within: Peacemaking in the East Coast of Nicaragua." Paper commissioned by George Fox College, under a grant from the United States Institute of Peace, Washington, D.C., 1989.

Lindgren, Karin, ed. *States in Armed Conflict*. Uppsala, Sweden: Department of Peace and Conflict Research, 1991.

Lunden, Suzanne, ed. *The Horn of Africa Bulletin*. Uppsala, Sweden: Life and Peace Institute, 1993.

———. "Working Document of the Life and Peace Institute on Somalia." Uppsala, Sweden: Life and Peace Institute, 1992.

Lusophone Consultation. "Peace and Reconciliation in Angola and Mozambique." Communiqué from participants, Limuru, Kenya, 20–27 September 1990.

Marchal, Roland. "Formes de la violence dans un espace urbain en guerre: Les Mooryaan de Mogadiscio." *Cahiers d'études Africaines* 117 (October 1993).

Mearsheimer, John J. "Back to the Future: Instability in Europe after the Cold War." *International Security* 15, no. 1 (summer 1990): 5–56.

Merton, Robert. *Social Theory and Social Structure*. Glencoe, Ill.: Free Press, 1949.

Midlarsky, Manus I. *The Internationalization of Communal Strife*. New York: Routledge, 1992.

Miller, Harold. *Peace and Reconcilaition in Africa*, Mennonite Central Committee Occasional Paper no. 19. Akron, Pa.: Mennonite Central Committee, July 1993.

Mitchell, Christopher. "External Peace-Making Initiatives and Intranational Conflict." In *The Internationalization of Communal Strife*, edited by Manus I. Midlarsky. New York: Routledge, 1992.

———. "The Process and Stages of Mediation: Two Sudanese Cases." *In Making War and Waging Peace: Foreign Intervention in Africa*, edited by David Smock. Washington, D.C.: United States Institute of Peace Press, 1993.

Moore, Christopher W. *Dispute Management Systems Design*. Boulder, Colo.: LDR Associates, 1994.

Montville, Joseph. *Conflict and Peacemaking in Multi-Ethnic Societies*. Lexington, Mass.: Lexington, 1990.

Mueller, John. *Retreat From Doomsday: The Obsolescence of Major War*. New York: Basic, 1989.

Nathan, Laurie. "An Imperfect Bridge: Crossing to Democracy on the Peace Accord." *Track Two* 2 (May 1993).

Nichols, Bruce. "Religious Conciliation between the Sandinistas and the East Coast Indians of Nicaragua." In *Religion: The Missing Dimension in Statecraft*, edited by Doug Johnston and Cynthia Sampson. Oxford: Oxford University Press, 1994.

Normark, Sture, Suzanne Lunden, and John Paul Lederach. "Blueprint: Somali Reconciliation Structure." Working paper, Life and Peace Institute, Uppsala, Sweden, 1993.

Parenti, Michael. *Inventing Reality: The Politics of the Mass Media*. New York: St. Martin's, 1990.

Regehr, Ernie. "Armed Conflict in the World in 1992." *Ploughshares Monitor* 8, no. 4 (December 1996): 13-17.

———. "Report on the Disarmament Resource Group." Frankfurt, December 1993.

———. *War after the Cold War: Shaping a Canadian Response*. Ploughshares Working Paper 93-3. Waterloo, Ontario: Project Ploughshares, 1993.

Richardson, Lewis. *Statistics of Deadly Quarrels*. Pittsburgh: Boxwood, 1960.

Rothman, Jay. "Action Evaluation: Draft Discussion Paper." March 1996.

———. *From Confrontation to Cooperation*. London: Sage, 1992.

Ruppesinghe, Kumar. *Conflict Transformation*. London: Macmillan, 1994.

Saunders, Harold H. *The Concept of Relationship*. Columbus: Ohio State University, Mershon Center, 1993.

Saunders, Harold H., and Randa Slim. "Dialogue to Change Conflictual Relationships." *Higher Education Exchange* (1994): 43–56.

Schultz, Beatrice. "Conflict Resolution Training Programs: Implications for Theory and Research." *Negotiation Journal* 5, no. 3 (1989): 301–309.

Seidman, Ann, and Anang Frederick. *Towards a New Vision of Self-Sustained Development.* Trenton, N.J.: Africa World Press, 1992.

Shenk, Gerald. 1993. *God with Us? The Role of Religion in Conflicts in the Former Yugoslavia.* Research Report no. 15. Uppsala, Sweden: Life and Peace Institute, 1993.

Sivard, Ruth Leger. *World and Social Expenditures.* Washington, D.C.: World Priorities, 1983.

Smith, Kenwin K., and David N. Berg. *Paradoxes of Group Life.* San Francisco: Jossey-Bass, 1987.

Spencer, Dayle, William Spencer, and William Ury, eds. *The State of World Conflict Report.* Atlanta: International Negotiation Network of the Carter Center, 1992.

Spencer, Dayle, and William Spencer. *The International Negotiation Network: A New Method of Approaching Some Very Old Problems.* Occasional Paper Series, vol. 2, no. 2. Atlanta: Carter Center, 1992.

Stockholm International Peace Research Institute Staff. *SIPRI Yearbook 1995: Armaments, Disarmament, and International Security.* Oxford: Oxford University Press, 1995.

Sun Tzu. *The Art of War.* Edited and translated by Thomas Cleary. New York: Shambhala, 1991.

Volkan, Vamik, Demetrios Julius, and Joseph Montville. *The Psychodynamics of International Relations.* Lexington, Mass.: Lexington, 1990.

Wallensteen, Peter. "Conflict Resolution after the Cold War: Five Implications." In *Resolving Intra-National Conflicts: A Strengthened Role for Intergovernmental Organizations,* edited by Honggang Yang, 34–42. Conference Report Series, vol. 5, no. 1. Atlanta: Carter Center, 1993.

Wallensteen, Peter and Karin Axell. "Armed Conflict at the End of the Cold War, 1989–1992." *Journal of Peace Research* 30, no. 3 (August 1993): 331–346.

Wehr, Paul, and John Paul Lederach. "Mediating Conflict in Central America." *Journal of Peace Research* 28, no. 1 (February 1991): 85–98.

Weiss, Carol. "Nothing as Practical as a Good Theory: Exploring Theory-Based Evaluation for Comprehensive Community Initiatives for Children and Families." In *New Approaches to Evaluating Community Initiatives,* edited by James P. Connell, Anne C. Kubisch, Lisbeth B. Schorr, and Carol Weiss. Washington, D.C.: Aspen Institute, 1995.

Wheatley, Margaret J. *Leadership and the New Sciences.* San Francisco: Berrett-Koehler, 1992.

Wright, Quincy. *A Study of War*. Chicago: University of Chicago Press, 1942.

Zehr, Howard. *Changing Lanes: New Perspectives on Crime and Punishment*. Scottdale, Pa.: Herald Press, 1990.

United States Institute of Peace

The United States Institute of Peace is an independent, nonpartisan federal institution created and funded by Congress to promote research, education, and training on the peaceful resolution of international conflicts. Established in 1984, the Institute meets its congressional mandate through an array of programs, including research grants, fellowships, professional training programs, conferences and workshops, library services, publications, and other educational activities. The Institute's Board of Directors is appointed by the President of the United States and confirmed by the Senate.

Chairman of the Board: Chester A. Crocker
Vice Chairman: Max M. Kampelman
President: Richard H. Solomon
Executive Vice President: Harriet Hentges

Board of Directors
Chester A. Crocker (Chairman), Research Professor of Diplomacy, School of Foreign Service, Georgetown University
Max M. Kampelman, Esq. (Vice Chairman), Fried, Frank, Harris, Shriver and Jacobson, Washington, D.C.
Dennis L. Bark, Senior Fellow, Hoover Institution on War, Revolution and Peace, Stanford University
Theodore M. Hesburgh, President Emeritus, University of Notre Dame
Seymour Martin Lipset, Hazel Professor of Public Policy, George Mason University
W. Scott Thompson, Professor of International Politics, Fletcher School of Law and Diplomacy, Tufts University
Allen Weinstein, President, Center for Democracy, Washington, D.C.
Harriet Zimmerman, Vice President, American Israel Public Affairs Committee, Washington, D.C.

Members ex officio
Richard A. Chilcoat, Lieutenant General, U.S. Army; President, National Defense University
Ralph Earle II, Deputy Director, U.S. Arms Control and Disarmament Agency
Phyllis Oakley, Assistant Secretary of State for Intelligence and Research
Walter B. Slocombe, Under Secretary of Defense for Policy
Richard H. Solomon, President, United States Institute of Peace (nonvoting)

John Paul Lederach is renowned both as a scholar and as a practitioner of conflict resolution. Founding director of the Conflict Transformation Program at Eastern Mennonite University, he has conducted numerous research projects with the Life and Peace Institute (Uppsala, Sweden), the Institute of Peace and Conflict Studies (Conrad Grebel College, Ontario), and the United States Institute of Peace, and has published extensively. His books include *Preparing for Peace: Conflict Transformation across Cultures* (1995) and *The Journey toward Reconciliation* (in press). As a practitioner, Lederach has spent fifteen years providing training and supporting peace-building initiatives in such places as Columbia, Somalia, The Philippines, Nicaragua, and Northern Ireland.

Under an executive fellowship of the United States Institute of Peace for 1997–98, John Prendergast is a director of African Affairs at the National Security Council (which he joined after writing his contribution to this book). For eight years, he directed the Horn of Africa Project at the Center of Concern, and he has been a visiting fellow at the University of Maryland. He has worked with a variety of relief and development NGOs, UN and government agencies, and human rights organizations. He is the author of numerous articles and several books on Africa, including *Front-line Diplomacy: Humanitarian Aid and Conflict in Africa* (1996), *Crisis Response: Humanitarian Band-Aids in Sudan and Somalia* (1997), and *Crisis and Hope in Africa* (1996).

BUILDING PEACE

This book is set in Adobe Caslon; the display type is Twentieth Century. Hasten Design Studio designed the book's cover, and Joan Engelhardt and Day Dosch designed the interior. Pages were made up by Helene Y. Redmond. Figures were prepared by Ken Allen. The book's editor was Nigel Quinney.